Quebec Lighthouses
by Harold Stiver

Copyright Statement

Quebec Lighthouses
A Guide for Photographers and Explorers

Published by Harold Stiver
Copyright 2025 Harold Stiver

Table of Contents

Tours

A Short History of Lighthouses

There is some evidence of a lighthouse from the 5th century B.C. of Themistocles of Athens constructing a stone column with a fire on top. This was at the harbour of Piraeus, associated with Athens.

However one of most famous and spectacular early structures was the Lighthouse of Alexandria, or the Pharos of Alexandria. It was one of the Seven Wonders of the Ancient World.

The lighthouse was built in the Third Century B.C. in Alexandria, Egypt by Ptolemy II. It stood on the island of Pharos in the harbour of Alexandria and was said to be 110 metres (350 feet) high.

The lighthouse was built in three stages, a large square at the bottom, an octagonal layer in the middle, and a cylindrical tower at the top.

The structure lasted until a series of earthquakes damaged it, with the 1303 Crete earthquake resulting in its destruction.

The Tower of Hercules, in northwest Spain, is modelled after the Pharos Lighthouse.

The first lighthouse in Canada was built in 1734 in Louisbourg on Cape Breton Island, Nova Scotia. Over the years, the structure was damaged beyond repair in a battle between the British and the French in 1758, destroyed by fire in 1923 and had to be rebuilt several times. The lighthouse known today was built in 1923.

Currently Canada's oldest surviving lighthouse is Sambro Island Lighthouse, built in 1758 at the entrance to Halifax Harbour. It is seen in the image above.

The oldest surviving lighthouse in Quebec is the Île Verte or Green Island Lighthouse which opened in 1809. It is situated on Notre-Dame-de-l'Isle-Verte in the St. Lawrence River. It is the third oldest surviving lighthouse in Canada.

It was built to aid mariners in this area which is subject to fog and currents in a place of dangerous reefs..

Quebec and Range Lights

Calvaire Range Lights

Range lights, also known as leading lights, are guides to navigation. Made up of a pair of lights used to aid ships along a specific path, particularly in channels with nearby obstructions such as reefs or shallows, or areas where a turn is needed. By aligning the vessel between them, the vessel can navigate safely.

As you become familiar with Quebec's lighthouses you quickly become aware of the large number of sets of range lights there are there. In fact Quebec contains more sets then any other province, any state or any other country with over 60% of its lighthouses being part of a range.

What is the reason for this? The answer lies in the provinces geography. The St. Lawrence River flows from Lake Ontario to the Gulf of St. Lawrence. It completely crossed Quebec from west to east on it's nearly 1,200 km. journey. At the same time there are a large number of obstacles in the river as well as areas where the channels change direction.

Following is a list of lights where at least one of the lights has survived.

Ange-Gardien Range	Ash Island Range Rear*
Baie Ellis Range*	Banc du Cap Brûlé Range
Barre à Boulard Range	Batiscan Range
Bécancour Range	Bouchard Peninsula Range
Calvaire Front Range*	Calvaire Range
Cap-aux-Corbeaux Range	Cap-de-la-Madeleine Range
Cap-de-la-Madeleine Wharf Range	Champlain Range
Contrecoeur-Verchères Range	Dixie Range*

Gallia Bay Lower Range
Gentilly Range
Île aux Raisins Range
Île Bouchard Range
Île des Barques Range
Île du Moine Range
Île Ste-Thérèse Lower Range
Îles de Varennes Range
Lachine Range
Leclercville Range
Montmagny Range
Petite Traverse Range
Pointe du Lac Range
Port Saint-François Range
Rivière Valin Range
Route Île Saint-Ours Range
Route Louiseville Upstream
Saint-Antoine Traverse Range
Sainte-Croix Range
Soulanges Lower Entrance Range
Traverse Cap-Santé Range
Traverse Longue-Pointe Range
Verchères Village Range

Gallia Bay Upper Range
Grondines Upper Range
Île aux Vaches Traverse Front Range
Île de Grâce Range
Île Deslauriers Range
Île Dupas Range
Île Ste-Thérèse Upper Range
La Pérade Range
Lavaltrie Range
Lotbinière Range
Mousseau Range
Pointe des Grondines Range
Pointe Noire Range
Portneuf Range
Route de Contrecoeur Range
Route Louiseville Downstream
Saint-Antoine Course Range
Sainte-Anne-de-Sorel
Saint-Michel Range
Soulanges Upper Entrance Range
Traverse Contrecoeur Range
Verchères Traverse

* single surviving lighthouse

Regional Map of Quebec

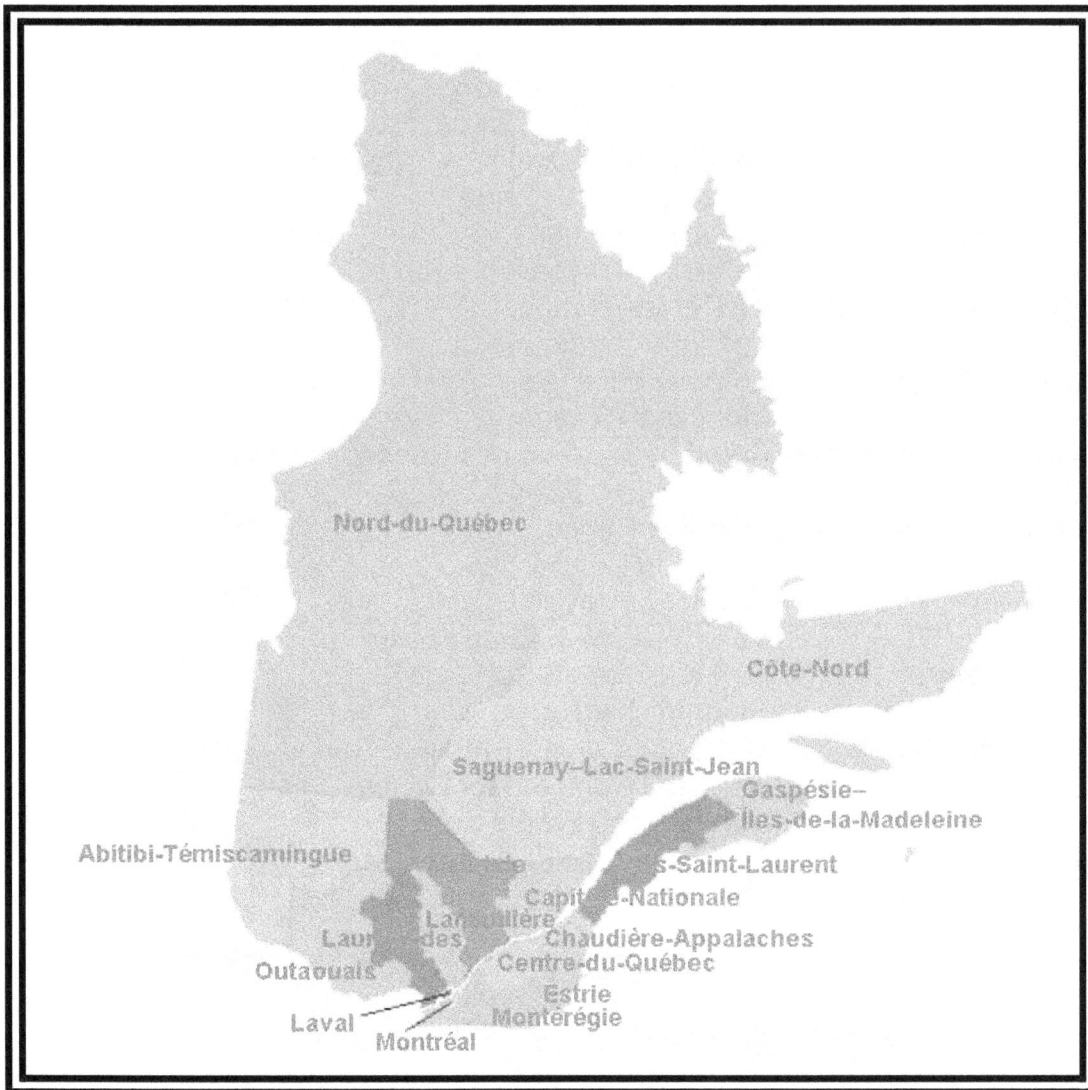

Ange-Gardien Range Lights

The Ange-Gardien Range Lights, Sainte-Famille Range Lights and Sainte-Pierre Range Lights were budgeted for in 1884 to aid mariners travelling the Orleans Channel. The contact for these six lighthouses was fulfilled by Nesbit and Auger, of Quebec and they opened in 1885. The Ange-Gardien Range Lights consisted of a tower for the front light and a pole for the rear light. In the early 1950s, the signal was changed from fixed white to fixed green which it remains today. In the 1990s the lights were replaced with the current skeleton towers.

Front Range (Image above)

Description: Skeleton tower

Location: Boischatel

Directions: From Boischatel, head SE on Côte de l'Église for 650 meters and turn left onto Rue Dugal. After 1.5 km, find the site

Coordinates: 46°54'08.2"N 71°07'06.2"W

Opened: Original 1885, Current 1994

Automated: 1923

Deactivated: Active

Height: 12 meters, 40 feet

Focal Height: 14.5 meters, 48 feet

Signal: Fixed Green

Visitor Access: Closed

Rear Range

Description: Skeleton tower

Location: Boischatel

Directions: From Boischatel, head SE on Côte de l'Église for 1.1 km and turn left on QC-138 E. In 500 meters turn right to find the site

Coordinates: 46°53'56.0"N 71°07'14.0"W

Opened: Original 1885, Current 1994

Automated: 1923

Deactivated: Active

Height: 13.5 meters, 45 feet

Focal Height: 24.5 meters, 81 feet

Signal: Fixed Green

Visitor Access: Closed

Ash Island Range Lights

Until the railways supplanted it, the Richelieu River was an important route from Lake Chanplain to the St. Lawrence. In 1871 requests were made for lights along this route. The Department of Marine budgeted funds for six lighthouses on the river and James Sheridan fulfilled this contract. The Ash Island Range Lights opened in 1875 with one light on Ash Island and the other on Bloody Island. A skeleton tower replaced the front light in 1913. The lights were deactivated in 2005 and there are no longer any active lighthouses on the river.

Front Range (Image above)

Description: Skeleton Tower

Location: Lacolle

Directions: Accessible by boat

Coordinates: 45°03'55.1"N 73°19'33.6"W

Opened: Original 1875, Current 1913

Automated: 1937

Deactivated: 2015

Height: 13 meters, 42 feet

Focal Height: 13.5 meters, 44 feet

Signal: Fixed white

Visitor Access: Grounds open, tower closed

Rear Range

Description: Skeleton Tower

Location: Lacolle

Directions: Accessible by boat

Coordinates: 45°03'34.2"N 73°19'41.4"W

Opened: Original 1875, Current 1913

Automated: 1937

Deactivated: 2015

Height: 20 meters, 66 feet

Focal Height: Not known

Signal: Fixed white

Visitor Access: Grounds open, tower closed

Baie Ellis Range Rear Lighthouse

In 1895, Henri Menier, a wealthy Swiss businessman purchased Anticosti Island for a private reserve as well as a business resource. He had a set of range lights built which opened in 1906. The government of Canada purchased the island in 1974 and decommissioned the lights in 1985.

Description: White, cylindrical iron tower

Location: Port Menier

Directions: From Port Meneir, head north on Chem. Martin-Zédé toward for 1.5 km and turn left onto Chemin de la Baie Ste Claire/Rue des Menier and the site is a short distance.

Coordinates: 49°49'30.5"N 64°22'31.3"W

Opened: 1906

Automated: Not known

Deactivated: 1986

Height: 16 meters, 52 feet

Focal Height: 24 meters, 79 feet

Signal: Fixed Green

Foghorn signal: N/A

Visitor Access: Grounds open, tower closed

Banc du Cap Brûlé Range Lights

In 1864 requests were made for a lighthouse for ships using the North Channel of the St. Lawrence River between Montée du Lac and Banc du Cap Brûlé and a light was opened in 1870. In 1931 the range lights opened with the lights atop concrete piers. The current towers replaced them in 1965. They were automated in 1969 and continue to be active.

Upstream Range

Description: Round cylindrical tower

Location: Sainte-Titte-des-Caps

Directions: Accessible by boat

Coordinates: 47°05'50.1"N 70°42'12.7"W

Opened: Original 1931, Current 1965

Automated: 1969

Deactivated: Active

Height: 20 meters, 65 feet

Focal Height: 23 meters, 76 feet

Signal: Fixed white

Foghorn Signal: N/A

Visitor Access: Grounds open, tower closed

Downstream Range (Image above)

Description: Round cylindrical tower

Location: Sainte-Titte-des-Caps

Directions: Accessible by boat

Coordinates: 47°05'22.8"N 70°42'38.7"W

Opened: Original 1931, Current 1965

Automated: 1969

Deactivated: Active

Height: 17 meters, 55 feet

Focal Height: 23 meters, 76 feet

Signal: Fixed white

Foghorn Signal: N/A

Visitor Access: Grounds open, tower closed

Barre à Boulard Range Lights

After a new channel was dredged downstream from Île Richelieu on the St. Lawrence River, the Barre à Boulard Range Lights were erected and opened in 1899. The front range light was an octagonal, wooden, pyramidal tower, while the rear end light was projected from a small building. In 1901 the signals were changed from fixed red to fixed white and the rear light was replaced by a skeleton tower. In 1916 the rear light became the front and a new rear light was built. In 1992 a skeleton tower replaced the rear light.

Front Range

Description: Skeleton Tower

Location: Lotbiniére

Directions: From Lotbiniére, head east on QC-132 E for 4.9 km and the site is on the left

Coordinates: 46°39'34.0"N 71°52'34.6"W

Opened: Original 1899, Current 1992

Automated: 1923

Deactivated: Active

Height: 18 meters, 61 feet

Focal Height: 52 meters, 170 feet

Signal: Fixed white

Visitor Access: Closed

Rear Range (Image above)

Description: Skeleton Tower

Location: Lotbiniére

Directions: From Lotbiniére, head east on QC-132 E for 5.9 km and the site is on the left.

Coordinates: 46°39'54.1"N 71°51'54.5"W

Opened: Original 1899, Current 1992

Automated: 1923

Deactivated: Active

Height: 20 meters, 66 feet

Focal Height: 71 meters, 233 feet

Signal: Fixed white

Visitor Access: Closed

Batiscan Range Lights

In 1884, the Batiscan Range Lights were erected to aid captains travelling south of Trois-Rivières where the Batiscan River flows into the St. Lawrence River. In 1908 new towers were built to replace them in new positions to mark the newly dredged channel. In 2012 the current skeleton towers where erected. They remain active with a fixed green signal.

Front Range

Description: Square skeleton tower

Location: Batiscan

Directions: From Le Marigot, head south on QC-138 O for 400 meters and turn left onto Rue du Phare and the site is 500 meters

Coordinates: 46°30'33.6"N 72°14'22.9"W

Opened: Original 1864, Current 2012

Automated: 1923

Deactivated: Active

Height: 8 meters, 26 feet

Focal Height: 17 meters, 55 feet

Signal: Fixed green

Visitor Access: Grounds open, tower closed

Rear Range (Image Above)

Description: Square skeleton tower

Location: Quebec City

Directions: From Le Marigot, head south on QC-138 O for 400 meters and turn left onto Rue du Phare and the site is 500 meters

Coordinates: 46°30'26.6"N 72°14'40.7"W

Opened: Original 1864, Current 2012

Automated: 1923

Deactivated: Active

Height: 14 meters, 46 feet

Focal Height: 17 meters, 55 feet

Signal: Fixed green

Visitor Access: Grounds open, tower closed

Bécancour Range Lights

The Bécancour Range Lights were erected in 1904 as an aid to vessels travelling the St. Lawrence River by the Bécancour River. The signals were originally fixed white, but later changed to fixed green. In 2009 the rear tower was replaced by a square skeleton tower. The lights continue to be active.

Front Range (Image above)

Description: Square tower

Location: Bécancour

Directions: From Bécancour. head NW on QC-132 O for 1.1 km and turn right onto Av. de l'Anse and the site is 1.7 km

Coordinates: 46°22'24.1"N 72°26'58.4"W

Opened: Original 1904, Current not known

Automated: 1923

Deactivated: Active

Height: 6.5 meters, 21 feet

Focal Height: 7 meters, 23 feet

Signal: Fixed green

Visitor Access: Grounds open, tower closed

Rear Range

Description: Square skeleton tower

Location: Bécancour

Directions: From Bécancour. head NW on QC-132 O for 2.2 km and turn right and the site is 650 meters

Coordinates: 46°21'46.7"N 72°28'03.1"W

Opened: Original 1904, Current 2009

Automated: 1923

Deactivated: Active

Height: 17 meters, 55 feet

Focal Height: 23 meters, 75 feet

Signal: Fixed green

Visitor Access: Grounds open, tower closed

Bon Désir Lighthouse

The Bon Désir Lighthouse was opened in 1941 to guide ships travelling the North Channel of the St. Lawrence River near its intersection with the Saguenay River. A foghorn was added shortly after. The current lighthouse was built by Euclide Tremblay and Camille Dufour and opened in 1957. The light continues to be active. The site operates as an interpretation centre for lighthouse information and marine life and it is is an excellent area for whales.

Description: Octagonal concrete tower

Location: Grandes-Bergeronnes

Directions: From Bon-Désir, head SW on Chem. du-Cap-de-Bon-Désir for 1.1 km to find the site

Coordinates: 48°16'17.8"N 69°28'11.0"W

Opened: Original 1941, Current 1957

Automated: 1982

Deactivated: Active

Height: 10.5 meters, 35 feet

Focal Height: 44.5 meters, 146 feet

Signal: White flash every 5 seconds

Foghorn signal: 5 second blast every 40 seconds

Visitor Access: Grounds open, tower closed

Cabano Lighthouse

Located at the south pier at the Cabano marina, it is privately owned by the town.

Description: Hexagonal tower

Location: Cabano

Directions: Viewable from Rue de la Plage in Cabano

Coordinates: 47°41'01.5"N 68°52'22.8"W

Opened: 1999

Automated: 1999

Deactivated: Active

Height: 13 meters, 43 feet

Focal Height: Not known

Signal: Fixed white

Foghorn Signal: N/A

Visitor Access: Grounds open, tower closed

Calvaire (Cap Charles) Front Range Light

In 1915 the Calvaire (Cap Charles) Range Lights were erected to aid mariners travelling on the St. Lawrence River east of Deschaillons-sur-Saint-Laurent. The front tower is inactive after being replaced by a skeleton tower in the 1980s. It was relocated to a municipal park and in 2013 was rehabilitated.

Description: Square pyramidal wood tower

Location: Deschsillons-sur-Saint-Laurent

Directions: From Deschaillons-sur-Saint-Laurent, head west on Rte Marie-Victorin/QC-132 O for 1.2 km and the site is on the right.

Coordinates: 46°32'53.3"N 72°07'55.9"W

Opened: 1915

Automated: Not known

Deactivated: 1980s

Height: 7 meters, 23 feet

Focal Height: 40 meters, 132 feet

Signal: Fixed white

Foghorn Signal: N/A

Visitor Access: Grounds open, tower closed

Calvaire (Cap Charles) Range Lights

In 1915 the Calvaire (Cap Charles) Range Lights were erected guide ships travelling on the St. Lawrence River east of Deschaillons-sur-Saint-Laurent. They were replaced by skeleton towers in 1994 and continue to be active.

Front Range (Image above)

Description: Skeleton tower

Location: Deschsillons-sur-Saint-Laurent

Directions: From Deschaillons-sur-Saint-Laurent, head NE on QC-132 E for 2.1 km and the site is on the right.

Coordinates: 46°33'22.0"N 72°05'10.9"W

Opened: Original 1915, Current 1994

Deactivated: Active

Height: 10 meters, 33 feet

Focal Height: 40 meters, 129 feet

Signal: Fixed green

Visitor Access: Closed

Rear Range

Description: Skeleton tower

Location: Deschsillons-sur-Saint-Laurent

Directions: From Deschaillons-sur-Saint-Laurent, head NE on QC-132 E for 1.5 km and turn right onto Chem. des Houde where the site is 350 meters.

Coordinates: 46°33'22.0"N 72°05'10.9"W

Opened: Original 1915, Current 1994

Deactivated: Active

Height: 20.5 meters, 67 feet

Focal Height: 54 meters, 177 feet

Signal: Fixed green

Visitor Access: Closed

Cap à l'Est Lighthouse

In 1909 the Cap à l'Est lighthouse was the last light built on the Saguenay River at a sharp turn downstream from the town of Saguenay. The original lighting equipment was a 6th order Fresnel lens which projected a white fixed signal. The site currently has a signal of a white flash every five seconds.

Description: Octagonal cylindrical concrete tower

Location: Sainte-Rose-du-Nord

Directions: From Saint-Fulgence, head east on QC-172 E for 15.8 km and turn right onto Chem. du Cap à l'Est. After 8.2 km you will see the site.

Coordinates: 48°22'33.1"N 70°42'20.1"W

Opened: 1909

Automated: 1917

Deactivated: Active

Height: 8 meters, 27 feet

Focal Height: 17 meters, 56 feet

Signal: White flash every 5 seconds

Foghorn Signal: N/A

Visitor Access: Grounds open, tower closed

Cap au Saumon (Cape Salmon)

Île aux Lièvres is located in the middle of the St. Lawrence River with ships able to travel through its north channel or south channel. In 1862 lighthouses had been built for the south channel and in 1894 the Cap au Saumon (Cape Salmon) Lighthouse was opened to guide vessels in the north channel. The site was built by Jean Morray and included a fog alarm building. A diaphone fog alarm upgraded the foghorn in 1917. The lighthouse was replaced by the current one in 1955 and continues to be active.

Description: Octagonal pyramidal tower

Location: Saint-Siméon

Directions: From Port-au-Saumon, head NE on QC-138 E for 2.9 km and turn right onto Chem. de Port au Persil. After 2.0 km turn right on an unnamed road and the site is 2.6 km

Coordinates: 47°46'13.8"N 69°54'21.4"W

Opened: 1894

Automated: 1980

Deactivated: Active

Height: 14 meters, 46 feet

Focal Height: 25 meters, 82 feet

Signal: 3 white flashes every 15 seconds

Foghorn Signal: Blast every 30 seconds

Visitor Access: Grounds open by permission, tower closed

Cap Blanc Lighthouse

The Cap Blanc Lighthouse overlooks the famous Percé Rock in the Gaspé. Unfortunately the natural arch in the rock collapsed in 2015. The original lighthouse was a square pyramidal wooden tower which opened in 1874. A foghorn was added to the site in 1877. The current lighthouse, a white, octagonal, reinforced-concrete tower, replaced it in 1915. The site was decommissioned in 1956.

Description: Octagonal concrete tower

Location: Percé

Directions: From White-Head-Percé, head NE on QC-132 O for 1.6 km and turn right on an unnamed road and the site is 300 meters walk to the west.

Coordinates: 48°30'04.9"N 64°13'06.4"W

Opened: Original 1894, Current 1915

Automated: Not known

Deactivated: 1956

Height: 7 meters, 24 feet

Focal Height: 47 meters meters, 154 feet

Signal: White flash every five seconds

Foghorn : Foghorn added in 1877

Visitor Access: Closed

Cap Chat Lighthouse

The St. Lawrence River narrows with Cap Chat to the south and Pointe des Monts to the north. In 1871 the Cap Chat Lighthouse was built to aid ships passing this dangerous point. The square, wooden tower was erected by A. Gingras. It was replaced in a better position by a similar smaller tower in 1875 and in 1884 it was moved back from the cliff because of erosion. The light was deactivated but re-lit while privately maintained.

Description: Square reinforced concrete tower

Location: Cap-Chat

Directions: From Del-Val, head SW on QC-132 O for 190 meters and turn right onto Rte du Phare and the site is 650 meters

Coordinates: 49°05'20.6"N 66°44'27.7"W

Opened: Original 1871, Second 1875, Current 1909

Automated: 1988

Deactivated: 2007 but re-lit and active

Height: 13.5 meters, 44 feet

Focal Height: 41.5 meters, 136 feet

Signal: White flash every 6 seconds

Foghorn Signal: 3 blasts every 60 seconds

Visitor Access: Grounds open, tower closed

Cap de la Madeleine Lighthouse

Ships travelling to the St. Lawrence River originally used Cap de la Madeleine to locate their position. A lighthouse was built at Cape de la Madeleine, after an initial delay due to storms, it opened in 1871. John A. Cameron fulfilled the contract to build it. Fog control equipment was added to the site in 1892. The current lighthouse opened in 1907 and the original was demolished. Today the site is a centre for tourists with a museum and restaurant.

Description: Round cylindrical cast iron tower

Location: Madeleine-Centre

Directions: From Madeleine-Centre, head east on QC-132 E for 2.0 km and turn left onto Rue du Phare and the site is 600 meters

Coordinates: 49°15'04.0"N 65°19'31.1"W

Opened: Original 1871, Current 1907

Automated: 1987

Deactivated: Active

Height: 11 meters, 37 feet

Focal Height: 44.5 meters, 146 feet

Signal: 3 white flashes every 27 seconds

Foghorn : Fog whistle added to site in 1892

Visitor Access: Grounds open, tower open from early June to mid-October

Cap de la Table Lighthouse

Anticosti Island lies at the mouth of the St. Lawrence River and has been the site of hundreds of shipwrecks. The Cap de la Table Lighthouse was erected in 1919 along with Cap De Rabast and Charleton Point Lighthouses. The site includes a fog alarm as well. The site was automated in 1970 and continues to be active.

Description: Octagonal concrete tower

Location: Port Menier

Directions: There is a long rough road to the site which may not be currently passable. Telephone 1-800-463-0863 for information.

Coordinates: 49°21'04.3"N 61°53'46.2"W

Opened: 1919

Automated: 1970

Deactivated: Active

Height: 12 meters, 40 feet

Focal Height: 34 meters, 112 feet

Signal: Red flash every 6 seconds

Foghorn signal: 2 blasts every 16.5 seconds

Visitor Access: Grounds open, tower closed

Cap de la Tête au Chien (Cape Dogs) Lighthouse

The Cap de la Tête au Chien (Cape Dogs) Lighthouse was built in 1909 to guide vessels travelling the north channel of the St. Lawrence River near Saint-Siméon. It was added after Brandy Pot Lighthouse and Long Pilgrim Lighthouse were built in 1862. A fog alarm building was included but it is no longer in service. The light continues to be active.

Description: Octagonal cylindrical concrete tower

Location: Saint-Siméon

Directions: Accessible by boat

Coordinates: 47°54'41.5"N 69°48'23.7"W

Opened: 1909

Automated: 1952

Deactivated: Active

Height: 11 meters, 37 feet

Focal Height: 63 meters, 207 feet

Signal: 2 white flashes every 5 seconds

Foghorn signal : Blast every fifty seconds

Visitor Access: Closed

Cap de Rabast (North Point) Lighthouse

Anticosti Island lies at the mouth of the St. Lawrence River and has been the site of hundreds of shipwrecks. The Cap De Rabast was erected in 1919 along with Cap de la Table Lighthouse and Charleton Point Lighthouses. The site includes a fog alarm as well. The site was automated in 1980 and continues to be active.

Description: Octagonal concrete tower

Location: Port-Menier

Directions: From Port-Menier, head NE on Rte Transanticostienne for 8.8 km and turn left on unnamed road and travel 11.3 km. Turn left on an unnamed road for 3.7 and the site

Coordinates: 49°57'05.8"N 64°08'57.4"W

Opened: 1919

Automated: 1980

Deactivated: Active

Height: 22 meters, 72 feet

Focal Height: 24 meters, 78 feet

Signal: 3 white flashes every 30 seconds

Foghorn Signal: 2 blasts every 75 seconds

Visitor Access: Grounds open, tower closed

Cap des Rosiers Lighthouse

The Cap des Rosiers Lighthouse is the tallest lighthouse in Canada. Cap des Rosiers has had a great many shipwrecks and the lighthouse was erected in 1858 to guide the turn from the Gulf of St. Lawrence into the St. Lawrence River. Charles François-Xavier Baby fulfilled the building contract. It was outfitted with a 1sr order Fresnel lens with a range of 26 km (16 miles). The original keepers dwelling was demolished and replaced by two new dwellings in 1956.The site was listed as a national historic site in 1974 and remains active.

Description: Round limestone tower

Location: Gaspé

Directions: From Cap-des-Rosiers, head SE on QC-132 E for 1.2 km and turn left on an unnamed road and the site is 100 meters

Coordinates: 48°51'20.9"N 64°12'02.2"W

Opened: 1858

Automated: 1981

Deactivated: Active

Height: 34 meters, 125 feet

Focal Height: 41.5 meters, 136 feet

Signal: White flash every 15 seconds

Foghorn signal: Blast every 60 seconds

Visitor Access: Grounds open, tower open mid-June through mid-September

Cap d'Espoir Lighthouse

A lighthouse was proposed for Cap d'Espoir as an aid to local fishermen. P. Carroll fulfilled the contact to build it and it was completed in 1873. New lighting equipment was installed in 1913 after a fire and a fog control building was added at the same time. The current concrete tower replaced the wood frame tower in 1939. The station continues to be active.

Description: Octagonal concrete tower

Location: Cap d'Espoir

Directions: From the town of Cap d'Espoir, head SE on Rte du Phare for 1.3 km to find the site

Coordinates: 48°25'08.0"N 64°19'05.2"W

Opened: Original 1873, Current 1939

Automated: 193

Deactivated: Active

Height: 14 meters, 46 feet

Focal Height: 25.5 meters, 84 feet

Signal: 4 white flashes every 30 seconds

Foghorn Signal: 2 blasts every 60 seconds

Visitor Access: Grounds open, tower closed

Cap Gaspé Lighthouse

The Cap Gaspé Lighthouse was erected in 1873 to guide ships entering Gaspé Bay. The station included a fog control building and dwelling and was built by Doolan & Cassidy. The tower and dwelling were destroyed in a fire and E. T. Nesbitt fulfilled the contract to build a wooden tower and dwelling which opened in 1892. The current tower opened in 1950. It was automated in 1972 and continues to be active.

Description: Octagonal concrete tower

Location: Gaspé

Directions: From the village of Cap-aux-Os, head east on QC-132 O for 3.4 km and turn right onto Bd de Grande-Grève. After 10.3 km, park at the end of the road and walk south for 2.5 km to the site. The walk is fairly strenuous

Coordinates: 48°44'57.0"N 64°09'49.5"W

Opened: Original 1873, Second 1892, Current 1950

Automated: 1972

Deactivated: Active

Height: 9 meters, 30 feet

Focal Height: 107 meters, 351 feet

Signal: White flash every 5 seconds

Foghorn Signal: Blast every 60 seconds

Visitor Access: Grounds open, tower closed

Cap-Alright (Île du Havre aux Maisons) Lighthouse

The Cap-Alright (Île du Havre aux Maisons) Lighthouse was erected in the Magdalen Islands in 1928. It is the smallest in the Magdalen Islands. This wooden frame design is widely used for its simplicity and low construction cost. In 2005 it was featured on a Canada Post stamp. It was listed as a Heritage Site in 2015.

Description: Square pyramidal wooded tower

Location: Cap-aux-Meules

Directions: From the Cap aux Meules ferry landing, turn right onto Chemin Principal (QC-199) and after 5 km, turn right onto Chemin de la Pointe Basse. Continue for 3.2 km and find the site.

Coordinates: 47°23'27.0"N 61°46'25.9"W

Opened: 1928

Automated: Not known

Deactivated: Active

Height: 8 meters, 27 feet

Focal Height: 24 meters, 79 feet

Signal: White flash every 5 seconds

Visitor Access: Grounds open, tower closed

Cap-aux-Meules (Étang-du-Nord) Lighthouse

The Cap-aux-Meules (Étang-du-Nord) Lighthouse opened in 1874 on Point Hérissée to guide ships by Dead Man's Island on the Îles de la Madeleine. A steam fog whistle was included at the site the same year. The current lighthouse was erected in 1987. It became inactive in 2015.

Description: White, circular fiberglass tower

Location: Cap-aux-Meules

Directions: From L'Étang-du-Nord, head north on Chem. des Caps for 1.2 km and turn left onto Chem. du Phare. After 1.1 km, park and walk a short distance west to the site

Coordinates: 47°23'05.2"N 61°57'34.0"W

Opened: Original 1874, Current 1987

Automated: 1965

Deactivated: 2015

Height: 11.5 meters, 38 feet

Focal Height: 28.5 meters, 93 feet

Signal: White flash every 5 seconds

Foghorn signal: 2 blasts every 60 seconds

Visitor Access: Grounds open, tower closed

Cap-aux-Oies (Goose Cape) Lighthouse

The Cap-aux-Oies (Goose Cape) Lighthouse was erected in 1876 on the north shore of the St. Lawrence River east of Baie-Saint-Paul. The site lighting was upgraded with a 4th order Fresnel lens in 1907. In 1927 a fog alarm building was constructed nearby. The current skeleton tower remains active.

Description: Skeleton tower

Location: Les Éboulements

Directions: From Cap-aux-Oies, head south on Rang de Cap aux Oies for 1.0 km to find the site

Coordinates: 47°29'17.6"N 70°13'53.3"W

Opened: Original 1876, Current Ca.1994

Automated: Not known

Deactivated: Active

Height: 9.5 meters, 31 feet

Focal Height: 16 meters, 52 feet

Signal: White flash every 6 seconds

Foghorn signal: 2 blasts every 60 seconds

Visitor Access: Grounds open, tower closed

Cap-de-la-Madeleine Range Lights

The Cap-de-la-Madeleine Range Lights were erected in 1843 on the northern shore of the St. Lawrence River near Trois-Rivières. The original towers were replaced by skeleton towers which continue to be active.

Lower Range (Image above)

Description: Skeleton Tower

Location: Trois-Rivières

Directions: From Sainte-Marthe-du-Cap, head NE on Rue Notre Dame E/QC-138 E for 1.2 km and the site

Coordinates: 46°23'36.2"N 72°27'44.8"W

Opened: Original 1843, Current 1906

Deactivated: Active

Height: 9 meters, 30 feet

Focal Height: 18.5 meters, 61 feet

Signal: Fixed Green

Visitor Access: Closed

Upper Range

Description: Skeleton Tower

Location: Trois-Rivières

Directions: From Sainte-Marthe-du-Cap, head NE on Rue Notre Dame E/QC-138 E for 2.4 km and turn left onto Rte de Red Mill S and the site is 650 meters

Coordinates: 46°24'01.4"N 72°27'17.0"W

Opened: Original 1843, Current 1906

Deactivated: Active

Height: 23 meters, 75 feet

Focal Height: 33 meters, 108 feet

Signal: Fixed Green

Visitor Access: Closed

Carleton Lighthouse

The Carleton Lighthouse, a replica of a 1911 lighthouse was erected by the local community. It shows a red flash every 5 seconds and continues to be active.

Description: Square pyramidal wood tower

Location: Carleton

Directions: From Carleton-sur-mer, head east on QC-132 O for 1 km and turn right onto Rte Du Camping. After 2.5 km continue onto Av. du Phare and the site

Coordinates: 48°05'12.2"N 66°07'27.5"W

Opened: 1984

Automated: 1984

Deactivated: Active

Height: 8 meters, 28 feet

Focal Height: 9 meters, 30 feet

Signal: Red flash every 5 seconds

Foghorn signal: N/A

Visitor Access: Grounds open, tower closed

Champlain Range Lights

The Champlain Range Lights were opened in 1904 to mark the channel from Citrouille Point by the Champlain River. The have been replaced with skeleton towers, the rear in 2010 and the front on an unknown dare. Both lights remain active.

Front Range

Description: Skeleton Tower

Location: Champlain

Directions: From Le Haut-de-Champlain head NE on QC-138 E for 450 meters and

Coordinates: 46°26'06.2"N 72°21'26.0"W

Opened: Original 1904, Current 2010

Automated: Not known

Deactivated: Active

Height: 8 meters, 26 feet

Focal Height: 14 meters, 46 feet

Signal: Fixed green

Visitor Access: Closed

Rear Range (Image above)

Description: Skeleton Tower

Location: Champlain

Directions: From Le Haut-de-Champlain, head NE on QC-138 E for 50 meters and the site is 200 meters north on foot

Coordinates: 46°26'05.2"N 72°21'47.2"W

Opened: Original 1904, Current 2010

Automated: Not known

Deactivated: Active

Height: 21.5 meters, 71 feet

Focal Height: 28.5 meters, 94 feet

Signal: Fixed green

Visitor Access: Grounds open, tower closed

Contrecoeur-Verchères Range Lights

In 1903, three sets of Range Lights were erected to guide vessels using a channel between Verchères and Contrecoeur. The Contrecoeur-Verchères Range Lights marked the eastern end and were used with the Verchères Traverse Range and the Contrecoeur Traverse Range. The Contrecoeur-Verchères Range Lights continue to be active.

Front Range (Image above)

Description: Square skeletal tower

Location: Contrecoeur

Directions: Accessible by boat

Coordinates: 45°51'55.5"N 73°15'06.7"W

Opened: Original 1903, Current not known

Automated: Not known

Deactivated: Active

Height: 7 meters, 23 feet

Focal Height: 10 meters, 31 feet

Signal: Fixed green

Foghorn Signal: N/A

Visitor Access: Grounds open, tower closed

Rear Range

Description: Square skeletal tower

Location: Contrecoeur

Directions: Accessible by boat

Coordinates: 45°52'43.3"N 73°14'16.1"W

Opened: Original 1903, Current not known

Automated: Not known

Deactivated: Active

Height: 16 meters, 52 feet

Focal Height: 19 meters, 62 feet

Signal: Fixed green

Foghorn Signal: N/A

Visitor Access: Grounds open, tower closed

Dixie Range Light

Dixie Range Lights opened in 1915 to mark the channel at the lower end of Lake St. Louis. There are recent reports **the tower may have been demolished** and replaced by a light on a mast.

Description: Square pyramidal steel skeletal tower

Location: Dorval

Directions: Accessible by boat

Coordinates: 45°25'58.3"N 73°43'32.5"W

Opened: 1915

Automated: 1915

Deactivated: 2018

Height: 26 meters, 85 feet

Focal Height: 25 meters, 82 feet

Signal: Flashing green

Foghorn signal: N/A

Visitor Access: Grounds open, tower closed

Escarpement Bagot (South Point) Lighthouse

The Escarpement Bagot (South Point) Lighthouse opened in 1871 on Anticosti Island, which has experienced a large number of shipwrecks. It was replaced in 1912 by a concrete tower with flying buttresses. This tower survives and was declared a Recognized Federal Heritage Building in 1991. The current tower opened in 1980 and continues to be active.

Description: Square cylindrical skeletal tower

Location: Port-Menier

Directions: Accessible by boat

Coordinates: 49°03'57.9"N 62°15'35.1"W

Opened: Original 1871, Second 1912, Current 1980

Automated: 1963

Deactivated: Active

Height: 15 meters, 50 feet

Focal Height: 19.5 meters, 64 feet

Signal: White flash every 6 seconds

Foghorn signal: Blast every 60 seconds

Visitor Access: Grounds open, tower closed

Gentilly Range Lights

In 1907 the Gentilly Range Lights were established just east of the town of Gentilly where the St. Lawrence River makes a large turn. In 1915 the rear light suffered a fire which necessitated the installation of a new lantern room and lighting equipment. The lights remain active.

Front Range

Description: Square wood tower

Location: Sorel-Tracy

Directions: Accessible by boat

Coordinates: 46°25'49.3"N 72°15'46.6"W

Opened: Original 1907, Current 1920

Automated: Not known

Deactivated: Active

Height: 6 meters, 19 feet

Focal Height: 12 meters, 39 feet

Signal: Fixed green

Foghorn Signal: N/A

Access: Grounds open, tower closed

Rear Range (Image above)

Description: Square skeleton tower

Location: Sorel-Tracy

Directions: Accessible by boat

Coordinates: 46°25'48.3"N 72°15'45.2"W

Opened: Original 1907, Current 2008

Automated: Not known

Deactivated: Active

Height: 24 meters, 79 feet

Focal Height: 31 meters, 103 feet

Signal: Fixed green

Foghorn Signal: N/A

Access: Grounds open, tower closed

Grondines Upper Range Lights

In 1904, the Grondines Upper Range Lights were erected to mark a newly dredged channel above Grondines. In 1909 these towers were replaced by a wooden front light and a skeleton tower rear light. These lights continue to be active.

Front Range

Description: Square skeleton tower

Location: Grondines

Directions: Accessible by boat

Coordinates: 46°35'06.5"N 72°05'51.9"W

Opened: 1904

Automated: Not known

Deactivated: Active

Height: 8 meters, 26 feet

Focal Height: 9 meters, 30 feet

Signal: White flash every 2 seconds

Access: Grounds open, tower closed

Rear Range (Image above)

Description: Square skeleton tower

Location: Grondines

Directions: From Grondines-Ouest, head west on QC-138 O for 750 meters and the site is on the right

Coordinates: 46°35'49.9"N 72°04'43.4"W

Opened: 1904

Automated: Not known

Deactivated: Active

Height: 14.5 meters, 48 feet

Focal Height: 29.5 meters, 97 feet

Signal: White flash every 2 seconds

Access: Closed

Haut-fond Prince (Prince Shoal) Lighthouse

In 1860, the Prince of Wales came to Canada to open the Victoria Bridge in Montreal and his ship ran into a shoal. It was later designated as Prince Shoal. In 1905, a Lightship was utilized to mark the Prince Shoal. In 1964 the hourglass formed Haut-fond Prince (Prince Shoal) Lighthouse was built. It continues to be active.

Description: Tower rising from circular keeper's house

Location: Tadoussac

Directions: Accessible by boat

Coordinates: 48°06'28.0"N 69°36'52.4"W

Opened: Original 1905, Current 1964

Automated: 1987

Deactivated: Active

Height: 14 meters, 45 feet

Focal Height: 25 meters, 83 feet

Signal: White flash every 2.5 seconds

Foghorn Signal: N/A

Visitor Access: Closed

Île aux Oeufs (Egg Island) Lighthouse

The Île aux Oeufs (Egg Island) Lighthouse was opened in 1871 to aid vessels travelling towards the entrance to the St. Lawrence River and the dangers of Egg Island (Île-aux-Oeufs). The contract for the site was fulfilled by J. B. Spence. A new tower replaced the original in 1877 as the original was considered unstable. The current tower replaced it in 1955. The site was automated in 1969 and became inactive in 2003.

Description: Octagonal concrete tower

Location: Port-Cartier

Directions: Accessible by boat

Coordinates: 49°37'19.5"N 67°10'32.4"W

Opened: Original 1871, Second 1877, Current 1955

Automated: 1969

Deactivated: 2003

Height: 11 meters, 36 feet

Focal Height: 18.5 meters, 61 feet

Signal: White flash every 6 seconds

Foghorn signal: N/A

Visitor Access: Grounds open, tower closed

Île aux Perroquets Lighthouse

The Île aux Perroquets Lighthouse was established in 1888 to aid ships travelling near the Perroquet Islands. The island is named for the french of Sea Parrot, which referred to the many Puffins found on the islands. A fog alarm was added to the site in 1918. The current tower and a new dwelling were erected in 1951. It was listed as a heritage lighthouse in 2014.

Description: White octagonal concrete tower

Location: Mingan

Directions: Accessible by boat

Coordinates: 50°13'14.2"N 64°12'22.9"W

Opened: Original 1888, Current 1951

Automated: 1978

Deactivated: Active

Height: 10.5 meters, 35 feet

Focal Height: 24 meters, 79 feet

Signal: White flash every 5 seconds

Foghorn Signal: Blast every 60 seconds

Visitor Access: Grounds open, tower closed

Île aux Raisins Range Lights

A square, wooden lighthouse was erected on Île aux Raisins in 1843 and in 1863 another tower was built to form a range. In 1903 a new skeleton tower replaced the rear tower. In 2020 both lights consisted of towers with orange daymarks. They remain active.

Front Range (Image above)

Description: Post carrying a daymark

Location: Sorel-Tracy

Directions: Accessible by boat

Coordinates: 46°06'10.8"N 72°57'52.4"W

Opened: Original 1843, Current 2020

Automated: Not known

Deactivated: Active

Height: 7 meters, 23 feet

Focal Height: 9.5 meters, 31 feet

Signal: Fixed green

Access: Grounds open, tower closed

Rear Range

Description: Post carrying a daymark

Location: Sorel-Tracy

Directions: Accessible by boat

Coordinates: 46°05'52.6"N 72°57'58.5"W

Opened: Original 1863, Current 2020

Automated: Not known

Deactivated: Active

Height: 23.5 meters, 77 feet

Focal Height: 27 meters, 89 feet

Signal: Fixed green

Access: Grounds open, tower closed

Île Bicquette Lighthouse

After numerous requests, the Île Bicquette Lighthouse was opened in 1844 to mark the island for ships travelling the St. Lawrence River. The site included the masonry tower, a keeper's dwelling, powder magazine storage shed and gun house. In 1883 the dwelling was replaced. A 3rd order Fresnel lens upgraded the lighting equipment in 1909. The site continues to be active.

Description: Round masonry tower

Location: Le Bic

Directions: Accessible by boat

Coordinates: 48°24'55.9"N 68°53'33.7"W

Opened: 1844

Automated: 1987

Deactivated: Active

Height: 22.5 meters, 74 feet

Focal Height: 34 meters, 112 feet

Signal: White flash every 6 seconds

Foghorn Signal: Blast every 60 seconds

Visitor Access: Grounds open, tower closed

Île Bouchard Range Lights

The Île Bouchard Range Lights were built in 1902 to mark a newly dredged channel between Verchères Point, at Verchères, and Cap St. Michel, at Varennes. The current towers replaced them with the front light moved to a new position. They remain active.

Front Range

Description: Square cylindrical skeletal tower

Location: Verchères

Directions: Accessible by boat

Coordinates: 45°47'56.4"N 73°20'40.5"W

Opened: Original 1902, Current not known

Automated: Not known

Deactivated: Active

Height: 16.5 meters, 54 feet

Focal Height: 22 meters, 73 feet

Signal: Fixed green

Foghorn signal: N/A

Visitor Access: Closed

Rear Range (Image above)

Description: Square cylindrical skeletal tower

Location: Verchères

Directions: Accessible by boat

Coordinates: 45°48'20.8"N 73°20'14.3"W

Opened: Original 1902, Current not known

Automated: Not known

Deactivated: Active

Height: 16.5 meters, 54 feet

Focal Height: 13 meters, 43 feet

Signal: Fixed green

Foghorn signal: N/A

Visitor Access: Closed

Île Brion Lighthouse

Île Brion had been the site of many shipwrecks over the years and in 1905 the Île Brion Lighthouse was built to mark the spot. E. F. Munro completed the contract. In 1906 the lighting was upgraded with a 3rd order Fresnel lens. The lighthouse was automated in 1967 and the outbuildings were demolished in 1972. The light continues to be active.

Description: Octagonal pyramidal wooden tower

Location: Cap-aux-Meules

Directions: Accessible by boat

Coordinates: 47°46'54.3"N 61°30'30.7"W

Opened: 1905

Automated: 1967

Deactivated: Active

Height: 14 meters, 45 feet

Focal Height: 40 meters, 131 feet

Signal: White flash every 3 seconds

Foghorn Signal: N/A

Visitor Access: Closed

Île de Grâce Range Lights

The Île de Grâce Range Lights were opened in 1905 to guide vessels travelling the channel near Sorel-Tracy. In 1928 the current front tower replaced the original which was being undermined by erosion of the river bank. It was placed farther from the rear light. Both lights continue to be active.

Front Range (Image above)

Description: Square pyramidal wood

Location: Sorel-Tracy

Directions: Accessible by boat

Coordinates: 46°04'08.4"N 73°02'59.8"W

Opened: Original 1905, Current 1928

Automated: 1964

Deactivated: Active

Height: 9 meters, 30 feet

Focal Height: 13 meters, 42 feet

Signal: Fixed green

Foghorn signal: N/A

Access: Grounds open, tower closed

Rear Range

Description: Square pyramidal skeleton

Location: Sorel-Tracy

Directions: Accessible by boat

Coordinates: 46°04'13.8"N 73°02'33.0"W

Opened: 1905

Automated: 1964

Deactivated: Active

Height: 16.5 meters, 54 feet

Focal Height: 22 meters, 73 feet

Signal: Fixed green

Foghorn signal: N/A

Access: Grounds open, tower closed

Île d'Entrée (Entry Island) Lighthouse

The Île d'Entrée (Entry Island) Lighthouse was opened in 1874 to mark the island. The original light was a square, wooden tower attached to the keeper's dwelling which had a fixed red light. It was replaced by a octagonal, wooden tower and relocated 600 meters from the original. The work was done by O. Tremblay and the signal was changed to fixed white. The current tower was erected in 1969 with a flashing white signal and was deactivated in 2015.

Description: Octagonal pyramidal wooden tower

Location: Cap-aux-Meules

Directions: From the ferry landing, head south on Chemin de la Gravel Point 1.6 km to find the site

Coordinates: 47°16'03.0"N 61°42'19.4"W

Opened: Original 1874, Second 1905, Current 1969

Automated: 1988

Deactivated: 2015

Height: 13.5 meters, 48 feet

Focal Height: 31.5 meters, 103 feet

Signal: White flash every 2.5 seconds

Foghorn : Fog alarm added in 1923

Visitor Access: Grounds open, tower closed

Île des Barques Range Lights

The Île des Barques Range Lights were opened in 1907 to aid mariners travelling the St. Lawrence River on the south side near Sainte-Anne-de-Sorel. The front range light is located on Île des Barques while the tear range is on Île du Moine. Around 2011 the rear range light was replaced by a white tower. Both lights remain active.

Front Range (Image above)	Rear Range
Description: square wood tower on pier	**Description:** round tower
Location: Sorel-Tracy	**Location**: Sorel-Tracy
Directions: Accessible by boat	**Directions**: Accessible by boat
Coordinates: 46°05'03.2"N 72°59'55.5"W	**Coordinates**: 46°05'15.3"N 72°59'42.2"W
Opened: 1907	**Opened**: Original 1907, Current 2011
Automated: Not known	**Automated**: Not known
Deactivated: Active	**Deactivated**: Active
Height: 5 meters, 18 feet	**Height**: 20 meters, 66 feet
Focal Height: 11.5 meters, 37 feet	**Focal Height**: 25 meters, 82 feet
Signal: Fixed green	**Signal**: Fixed green
Visitor Access: Grounds open, tower closed	**Visitor Access:** Grounds open, tower closed

Île du Corossol Lighthouse

The Île du Corossol Lighthouse opened in 1870 as an aid to Captains travelling to the harbour off Sept-Iles which has multiple islands at its entrance. The construction was handled by Andrew Gingras. This building was lost to a fire in 1872. A replacement was built by R. Cameron and opened in 1876. A fog control building was added to the site in 1906. An octagonal, concrete lighthouse replaced it in 1953, built by Continental Construction. Finally the current skeleton tower was built in 1988 and remains active.

Description: Skeleton tower

Location: Sept-Iles

Directions: Accessible by boat

Coordinates: 50°05'24.5"N 66°22'39.0"W

Opened: Original 1870, Second 1876, Third 1953, Current 1988

Automated: 1985

Deactivated: Active

Height: 18 meters, 60 feet

Focal Height: Not known

Signal: White flash every 5 seconds

Foghorn: Fog alarm building added in 1906

Visitor Access: Closed

Île du Grand Caouis Lighthouse

The original Île du Grand Caouis Lighthouse opened in 1927 to guide boats to anchorage at Great Cawee Island. It comprised a square dwelling with a tower rising from its centre. The current lighthouse replaced the original in 1955. It was constructed by M. Cauvier and J. Keays and continues to be active.

Description: Octagonal concrete tower

Location: Port-Cartier

Directions: Accessible by boat

Coordinates: 49°49'39.9"N 67°00'24.3"W

Opened: Original 1927, Current 1955

Automated: 1970

Deactivated: Active

Height: 19 meters, 33 feet

Focal Height: 45 meters, 148 feet

Signal: White flash every 6 seconds

Foghorn: Acetylene canon (Unique to this site)

Visitor Access: Closed

Île du Havre-Aubert (Amherst Island) Lighthouse

The Îles de la Madeleine is located in the Gulf of St. Lawrence and has been a dangerous area for ships with over 200 wrecks recorded. The Île du Havre-Aubert Lighthouse was opened in 1871 on Amherst Island to aid mariners in the area . The construction contract was fulfilled by E. Chanteloup. Wires were attached to the tower in 1874 to stabilize it. The light was deactivated in 2011.

Description: Hexagonal wooden tower

Location: Cap-aux-Meules

Directions: From L'Anse-à-la-Cabane, head west on Chem. du Bass. toward for 1.2 km and turn left onto Chem. du Phare where the site is 400 meters

Coordinates: 47°12'44.5"N 61°58'18.7"W

Opened: 1871

Automated: 1970

Deactivated: 2011

Height: 16.5 meters, 64 feet

Focal Height: 31 meters, 102 feet

Signal: 3 white flashes every 20 seconds

Foghorn Signal: N/A

Visitor Access: Grounds open, tower closed

Île du Moine Range Lights

The Île du Moine Range Lights opened in 1906 to aid vessels travelling the St. Lawrence River between the Île de Grâce Range and Sainte-Anne-de-Sorel Range. At an unknown date the rear tower was replaced by the current skeleton tower. Both lights continue to be active.

Front Range (Image above)

Description: Square wood tower on pier

Location: Sorel-Tracy

Directions: Accessible by boat

Coordinates: 46°03'58.3"N 73°01'29.8"W

Opened: 1906

Automated: Not known

Deactivated: Active

Height: 5 meters, 18 feet

Focal Height: 13 meters, 43 feet

Signal: Fixed green

Foghorn Signal: N/A

Visitor Access: Grounds open, tower closed

Rear Range

Description: Skeleton tower on pier

Location: Sorel-Tracy

Directions: Accessible by boat

Coordinates: 46°03'27.4"N 73°09'22.9"W

Opened: Original 1906, Current not known

Automated: Not known

Deactivated: Active

Height: 18.5 meters, 57 feet

Focal Height: 27.5 meters, 90 feet

Signal: Fixed green

Foghorn Signal: N/A

Visitor Access: Grounds open, tower closed

Île Dupas Range Lights

There are a large number of islands in the St. Lawrence River across from Sorel-Tracy and in 1907 the Île Dupas Range Lights were established to guide ships. The rear range light was situated on Île Dupas while the front light was on Île aux Cochons. At some point a skeleton tower replaced the rear light. The signal was changed to fixed green in 1950 and both lights remain active.

Front Range

Description: Square wood tower on pier

Location: Sorel-Tracy

Directions: Accessible by boat

Coordinates: 46°03'27.4"N 73°09'22.9"W

Opened: 1907

Automated: Not known

Deactivated: Active

Height: 5 meters, 18 feet

Focal Height: 14 meters, 46 feet

Signal: Fixed green

Visitor Access: Grounds open, tower closed closed

Rear Range (Image above)

Description: Square skeleton tower

Location: Sorel-Tracy

Directions: From La Visitation-de-l'Île-Dupas, head south on Rang de l'Île to find the site

Coordinates: 46°03'47.2"N 73°09'15.1"W

Opened: Original 1907, Current not known

Automated: Not known

Deactivated: Active

Height: 20.5 meters, 67 feet

Focal Height: 25.5 meters, 84 feet

Signal: Fixed green

Visitor Access: Grounds open, tower

Île Greenly Lighthouse

Île Greenly lies at the east end of the Gulf of St. Lawrence near the Labrador shore. The Île Greenly Lighthouse was built in 1878 to mark this spot by James Mowat. In 1906 the lighting was upgraded with a 2nd order Fresnel lens. The original lighthouse was lost to a 1947 fire and a replacement opened later that year. The current tower opened in 1983 when the site was automated. It remains active.

Description: Trapezoidal pyramidal skeletal tower

Location: Blanc-Sablon

Directions: Accessible by boat

Coordinates: 51°22'29.2"N 57°11'26.4"W

Opened: Original 1878, Second 1947, Current 1983

Automated: 1983

Deactivated: Active

Height: 22 meters, 72 feet

Focal Height: 35 meters, 115 feet

Signal: White flash every 15 seconds

Foghorn signal: Blast every 60 seconds

Visitor Access: Grounds open, tower closed

63

Île Plate Lighthouse

The Île Plate Lighthouse opened in 1913 as an aid to vessels travelling the Gulf of St. Lawrence near the northern shore. It was lit by a 3rd order Fresnel lens. Note there is also a lighthouse called Île Plate on the Gaspe. A skeleton tower replaced it in 1979 when the light was automated. It became inactive in 2014.

Description: Hexagonal cylindrical concrete tower

Location: Mutton Bay

Directions: Accessible by boat

Coordinates: 50°45'12.4"N 58°45'20.9"W

Opened: Original 1913, Current 1979

Automated: 1979

Deactivated: 2014

Height: 24 meters, 80 feet

Focal Height: 22.5 meters, 74 feet

Signal: Fixed white

Foghorn signal: N/A

Visitor Access: Closed

Île Plate (Percé) Lighthouse

The Île Plate (Percé) Lighthouse in Gaspé, opened in 1883 on an island known as Flat Rock or Île Plate. It was built by James Desmond. Note there is a lighthouse in the Gulf of St. Lawrence also named Île Plate. A new wooden lighthouse replaced it in 1924. The current tower, a skeleton tower, replaced it in about 1952. It continues to be active.

Description: Square cylindrical skeletal tower

Location: Percé

Directions: Accessible by boat

Coordinates: 48°37'37.3"N 64°09'22.7"W

Opened: Original 1883, Second 1924, Current Ca.1952

Automated: Ca.1952

Deactivated: Active

Height: 15 meters, 49 feet

Focal Height: 20.5 meters, 67 feet

Signal: White flash every 6 seconds

Foghorn signal: N/A

Visitor Access: Closed

Île Richelieu Lighthouse

The Île Richelieu Lighthouse was opened in 1816 as a warning about the dangerous Richelieu Rapids on the St. Lawrence River. Three women, Helene Blais, Catherine Blais, and Julie Blais, acted as keepers between 1861 and 1890. In 1874 the lantern room was enlarged to accommodate larger lighting equipment. The light is still active.

Description: Conical concrete block tower

Location: Deschambault

Directions: Accessible by boat

Coordinates: 46°38'33.5"N 71°54'35.2"W

Opened: Original 1816, Current 1971

Automated: Not known

Deactivated: Active

Height: 6 meters, 19 feet

Focal Height: 6 meters, 19 feet

Signal: Fixed green

Foghorn Signal: N/A

Visitor Access: Grounds open, tower closed

Île Rouge (Red Island) Lighthouse

Due to a large number of shipwrecks in the lower part of the St. Lawrence River, requests were made for lighthouses to be added to that region. The Île Rouge (Red Island) Lighthouse was opened in 1848 to address these needs. Joseph Archer received the contract but it was finished by William Smith. The tower has three stringcourses which prevent water from running down the tower as well as being a pleasing design element. In 1871 a Lightship moored nearby, The lighthouse was staffed until 1988, one of the last to be automated.

Description: Cylindrical limestone tower

Location: Tadoussac

Directions: Accessible by boat

Coordinates: 48°04'10.0"N 69°33'16.9"W

Opened: 1848

Automated: 1988

Deactivated: Active

Height: 19.5 meters, 64 feet

Focal Height: 20 meters, 65 feet

Signal: White flash every 10 seconds

Foghorn: Fog control building added 1945

Visitor Access: Grounds open, tower closed

Île Sainte-Hélène Lighthouse

Île Sainte-Hélène is a large island on the St. Lawrence River, just downstream from the port of Montreal. The Île Sainte-Hélène Lighthouse opened in 1912 as the Rear range light of Ile Ronde Range. When the Front Range was discontinued, it became part of the La Ronde Amusement Park and known as Île Sainte-Hélène Lighthouse.

Description: White, square pyramidal concrete tower on concrete base

Location: Montreal

Directions: From Montreal, take QC-134 and Jacques Cartier Bridge to Île Sainte-Hélène. Take at Parc Jean-Drapeau and continue to La Ronde amusement park. The lighthouse is in the parking lot.

Coordinates: 45°31'06.9"N 73°32'17.6"W

Opened: 1907

Automated: Not known

Deactivated: 1950s

Height: 14.5 meters, 48 feet

Focal Height: Not known

Signal: Fixed white

Foghorn Signal: N/A

Visitor Access: Grounds open, tower closed

Île Sainte-Marie Lighthouse

The Île Sainte-Marie Lighthouse opened in 1913 as a guide to mark the St. Mary Island and Harrington Harbour. The image shown is this historic original lighthouse. A fog control building was added in 1921. The light was replaced by a skeleton tower in 1981 erected near the original light. The island is a sanctuary for nesting birds.

Description: Square skeletal tower

Location: Chevery

Directions: Accessible by boat

Coordinates: 50°18'15.0"N 59°39'23.5"W

Opened: Original 1913, Current 1981

Automated: 1981

Deactivated: Active

Height: 16.5 meters, 54 feet

Focal Height: 42 meters, 148 feet

Signal: White flash every 2.5 seconds

Foghorn Signal: Blast every 60 seconds

Visitor Access: Closed

Île Ste-Thérèse Upper Range

The Île Ste-Thérèse Upper Range Lights were established in 1879 to guide vessels travelling a new channel at Point aux Trembles. The contract was fulfilled by J. Sheridan. Both towers were re-positioned in 1884. Currently the back light is a square skeleton tower and the front is a white cylindrical tower. They both remain active.

Front Range

Description: Round cylindrical concrete

Location: Varennes

Directions: Accessible by boat

Coordinates: 45°40'29.9"N 73°27'33.8"W

Opened: Original 1879, Current not known

Automated: Not known

Deactivated: Active

Height: 12 meters, 39 feet

Focal Height: 11 meters, 36 feet

Signal: Fixed green

Foghorn Signal: N/A

Access: Grounds open, tower closed

Rear Range

Description: square skeleton mast on pier

Location: Varennes

Directions: Accessible by boat

Coordinates: 45°40'29.9"N 73°27'33.8"W

Opened: Original 1879, Current not known

Automated: Not known

Deactivated: Active

Height: 22 meters, 72 feet

Focal Height: 27 meters, 89 feet

Signal: Fixed green

Foghorn Signal: N/A

Access: Grounds open, tower closed

Île Verte (Green Island) Lighthouse

The Île Verte (Green Island) Lighthouse was opened in 1809 to mark the area around the island which had been a dangerous area with many shipwrecks. It was the first on the St. Lawrence River and the third in Canada. New dwellings were built in 1960. which now are available to rent. It was listed as a National Historic Site of Canada in 1974 and remains active.

Description: White cylindrical stone tower

Location: L'Isle Verte

Directions: From the ferry dock, turn left and then almost immediately right on the road to the lighthouse. The site is 2.5 km.

Coordinates: 48°03'04.0"N 69°25'27.0"W

Opened: 1809

Automated: 1972

Deactivated: Active

Height: 17 meters, 55 feet

Focal Height: 16.5, 54 feet

Signal: White flash every 5 seconds

Foghorn Signal: Cannon fired every 30 minutes

Access: Grounds open, tower closed

Îles de Varennes (Île a l'Aigle) Range Lights

The Îles de Varennes (Île a l'Aigle) Range Lights were established in 1903 to mark the newly dredged channel in Varennes Traverse. In 1967 the lights were replaced with skeleton towers. The current skeleton towers were opened in the 1980s..

Front Range

Description: Skeleton tower

Location: Varennes

Directions: Accessible by boat

Coordinates: 45°40'03.2"N 73°27'23.5"W

Opened: Original 1903, Current 1980s

Automated: 1967

Deactivated: Active

Height: Not known

Focal Height: Height: Not known

Signal: Fixed white

Foghorn signal: N/A

Access: Grounds open, tower closed

Rear Range (Image above)

Description: Skeleton tower

Location: Varennes

Directions: Accessible by boat

Coordinates: 45°40'03.2"N 73°27'23.5"W

Opened: Original 1903, Current 1980s

Automated: 1967

Deactivated: Active

Height: 16 meters, 52 feet

Focal Height: Height: 16 meters, 52 feet

Signal: Fixed white

Foghorn signal: N/A

Access: Grounds open, tower closed

La Martre Lighthouse

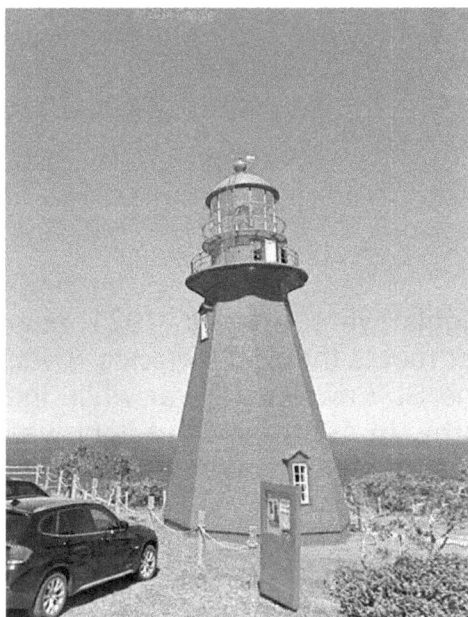

The original La Martre Lighthouse was opened in 1876 to mark the Gaspé Peninsula for ships travelling the entrance to the Gulf off St. Lawrence. The site included a fog control building. The current tower was built in 1906 and is painted bright red with a white vertical stripe. The site contains a town hall and museum at present. La Martre Lighthouse was listed as a Recognized Federal Heritage Building in 1988.

Description: Octagonal pyramidal wood tower

Location: La Martre

Directions: From La Marte, head west on Av. du Phare from Rte 132 for 280 meters to find the site

Coordinates: 49°12'22.1"N 66°10'16.8"W

Opened: Original 1876, Current 1906

Automated: 1972

Deactivated: Active

Height: 19 meters, 63 feet

Focal Height: 39.5 meters, 130 feet

Signal: 4 white flashes every 39 seconds

Foghorn signal: Blast every 60 seconds

Visitor Access: Grounds open, tower open mid June through early September

La Pérade Range Lights

The La Pérade Range Lights were opened 1921 near where the Sainte-Anne River meets the St. Lawrence River. The front was situated in the St. Lawrence River while the rear was on the shore nearby. In 1929 the front light was replaced and relocated to a skeleton tower. Both lights continue to be active.

Front Range

Description: Yellow skeleton tower

Location: Sainte-Anne-de-la-Pérade

Directions: Accessible by boat

Coordinates: 46°34'02.9"N 72°10'23.8"W

Opened: 1929

Automated: 1929

Deactivated: Active

Height: 6 meters, 20 feet

Focal Height: Not known

Signal: Fixed Green

Visitor Access: Grounds open, tower closed

Rear Range (Image above)

Description: Skeleton tower

Location: Sainte-Anne-de-la-Pérade

Directions: From Sainte-Anne-de-la-Pérade, head SE on Rue Sainte-Anne for 1.4 km and the site

Coordinates: 46°34'05.1"N 72°11'19.9"W

Opened: 1921

Automated: 1921

Deactivated: Active

Height: 26 meters, 85 feet

Focal Height: 26.5 meters, 88 feet

Signal: Fixed Green

Visitor Access: Private (Viewable from road)

Lachine Range Lights

The Lachine Rapids in Montreal were a barrier to ships, necessitating unloading and reloading cargo until the Lachine Canal opened in 1825. With the canal available, large ships could sail from the Atlantic to the Great Lakes. In 1889 a pair of pole lights were erected and in 1900 they were replaced by the current towers. Both lights were listed as Recognized Federal Heritage Buildings in 1991. They remain active.

Front Range

Description: Steel tower

Location: Lachine

Directions: In Montreal, head south to Parc Saint-Louis off Bd Saint-Joseph and walk the pier

Coordinates: 45°25'56.1"N 73°41'41.7"W

Opened: Original 1889, Current 1900

Automated: Not known

Deactivated: Active

Height: 7 meters, 24 feet

Focal Height: 9 meters, 30 feet

Signal: Fixed green

Visitor Access: Grounds open, tower closed

Rear Range (Image above)

Description: Steel tower

Location: Lachine

Directions: In Montreal, head south from 3045 Bd Saint-Joseph and find the site

Coordinates: 45°25'59.5"N 73°41'28.0"W

Opened: Original 1889, Current 1900

Automated: Not known

Deactivated: Active

Height: 17 meters, 55 feet

Focal Height: 18 meters, 59 feet

Signal: Fixed green

Visitor Access: Grounds open, tower closed

Leclercville (St. Emmélie) Range Lights

The Leclercville (St. Emmélie) Range Lights were completed by A. Cameron in 1880. However due to delays in completing the Cap à la Roche Channel, they were not lit until 1898. In 1915 skeleton towers replaced the original wooden towers. In 1983 the front range was moved from the cliff due to erosion. The current skeleton towers replaced the front and back range in 2002 and 2008 respectively.

Front Range (Image above)

Description: Square skeleton tower

Location: Leclercville

Directions: Located beside QC 132 about 2 km southwest of Leclercville

Coordinates: 46°33'44.6"N 72°00'49.0"W

Opened: Original 1898, Current 2002

Automated: Not known

Deactivated: Active

Height: 10 meters, 33 feet

Focal Height: 37 meters, 121 feet

Signal: Fixed green

Visitor Access: Grounds open, tower closed

Rear Range

Description: Square skeleton tower

Location: Leclercville

Directions: Located 1042 meters (0.6 mi) east of the front light.

Coordinates: 46°33'43.2"N 71°59'58.5"W

Opened: Original 1898, Current 2005

Automated: Not known

Deactivated: Active

Height: 11 meters, 36 feet

Focal Height: 57 meters, 186 feet

Signal: Fixed green

Visitor Access: Closed

Long Pèlerin (Long Pilgrim) Lighthouse

On the south shore of St. Lawrence River, south of Rivière-du-Loup lie the Pilgrim Islands. The Province of Canada budgeted for 5 lighthouses in the area including one for Long Pilgrim Island. Louis Dery completed the contract and the Long Pèlerin (Long Pilgrim) Lighthouse opened in1862. It included a 9 meter (30 foot) circular brick tower, as well as a keeper's dwelling and storerooms. It was replaced by a skeleton tower which was built next to the surviving original tower

Description: Square skeleton tower

Location: Saint-André

Directions: Accessible by boat

Coordinates: 47°42'58.8"N 69°44'51.8"W

Opened: Original 1862, Current 1982

Automated: 1967

Deactivated: Active

Height: 14 meters, 45 feet

Focal Height: 43.5 meters, 142 feet

Signal: White flash every 6 seconds

Foghorn Signal: N/A

Visitor Access: Grounds open, tower closed

Lotbinière Range Lights

Requests for lights in the Lotbinière were made as ships traffic was increasing in that region of the St. Lawrence River. J. Sheridan fulfilled a contract for range lights and they opened in 1871. In 1920 the front light was replaced by a skeleton tower and in 1993 a skeleton tower replaced the rear range. In 2006 the current front tower replaced the front light.

Front Range (Image above original tower)

Description: Square skeletal mast

Location: Lotbinière

Directions: From La Vieille-Église, head SW on QC-132 O for 150 meters and turn right Chem. de la Vieille Église and the site

Coordinates: 46°36'40.2"N 71°57'21.4"W

Opened: Original 1871, Current 2006

Automated: Not known

Deactivated: Active

Height: 12.5 meters, 41 feet

Focal Height: 15 meters, 50 feet

Signal: Fixed white

Visitor Access: Closed

Rear range

Description: Square cylindrical skeletal tower

Location: Lotbinière

Directions: From La Vieille-Église, head SW on QC-132 O for 1.0 km. and turn right on onto Falaise Morissette and see the site

Coordinates: 46°36'18.7"N 71°57'46.3"W

Opened: Original 1871, Current 1993

Automated: Not known

Deactivated: Active

Height: 17 meters, 56 feet

Focal Height: 41 meters, 135 feet

Signal: Fixed white

Visitor Access: Closed

Maskinongé Curve Lighthouse

Lake Saint-Peter is a lake on the St. Lawrence River between Trois-Rivières and Sorel-Tracy. In 1973 the Maskinongé Curve Lighthouse was erected to guide vessels at what is know as Curve 1 on the lake.

Description: Cylindrical tower

Location: Maskinongé

Directions: Accessible by boat

Coordinates: 46°09'24.4"N 72°56'28.6"W

Opened: 1973

Automated: 1973

Deactivated: Active

Height: 14 meters, 46 feet

Focal Height: 14 meters, 46 feet

Signal: Fixed yellow

Foghorn signal: N/A

Visitor Access: Grounds open, tower closed

Matane Lighthouse

The Matane Lighthouse was opened in 1873 to guide ships between Poine-au-Père Lighthouse and Cap Chat Lighthouse. It was built by S. Cimon. Due to erosion, the tower was moved 30 meters from the coast in 1894. A reinforced concrete cylindrical tower replaced the tower in 1907. It currently serves as an information centre and a museum. It was given an extensive restoration in 2019.

Description: Round cylindrical cast iron tower

Location: Matane

Directions: In Matane, the site is off the intersection of Le Cap-des-Pilotes and BD Dion.

Coordinates: 48°50'59.8"N 67°32'57.5"W

Opened: Original 1873, Current 1907

Automated: N/A

Deactivated: 1951

Height: 20 meters, 67 feet

Focal Height: Not known

Signal: 2 white flashes revere 7.5 seconds

Foghorn Signal: N/A

Visitor Access: Grounds open, tower open early June to mid-October

Montmagny Range Lights

The Montmagny Range Lights were opened in 1886 with a mast light on a square base on the wharf and a back light on an open wood frame. Square skeleton towers replaced them in 1933.

Front Range (Image above)

Description: Skeleton Tower

Location: Montmagny

Directions: In Montmagny, head NE on Rue du Manoir and a quick left onto Av. du Sault to the wharf and the site

Coordinates: 46°59'11.3"N 70°33'06.4"W

Opened: Original 1886, Current 1933

Automated: Not known

Deactivated: Active

Height: 6.5 meters, 31 feet

Focal Height: 8 meters, 26 feet

Signal: Fixed red

Visitor Access: Grounds open, tower closed

Rear Range

Description: Skeleton Tower

Location: Montmagny

Directions: In Montmagny, head NE on Rue du Manoir and a quick left onto Av. du Sault for 50 meters and site viewable from road

Coordinates: 46°59'08.5"N 70°33'05.4"W

Opened: Original 1886, Current 1933

Automated: Not known

Deactivated: Active

Height: Not known

Focal Height: Not known

Signal: Fixed red,

Visitor Access: Closed

Nicolet Sector Lighthouse

The Nicolet Sector Lighthouse opened in 1907 as the front range of a set of range lights erected near the mouth of the Nicolet River. In 1970 the rear light was discontinued and the front range became a sector light. It continues to be active.

Description: Square tower

Location: Nicolet

Directions: Accessible by boat

Coordinates: 46°15'27.1"N 72°39'03.5"W

Opened: Original 1907, Current 1938

Automated: Not known

Deactivated: Active

Height: 9 meters, 29 feet

Focal Height: 9 meters, 29 feet

Signal: White and Green light every 2 seconds

Foghorn Signal: N/A

Visitor Access: Grounds open, tower closed

Passage Lower Lighthouse

In 1887 the original Passage Lower Lighthouse was erected on L'Isle-aux-Allumettes on the Ottawa River as a guide to the narrow Lower Narrows. In 1907 it was replaced by a wooden tower built by F. Castle. The current tower is a replica built in 2021 of the 1907 lighthouse which had removed in 2020.

Description: Square pyramidal tower

Location: L'Isle-aux-Allumettes

Directions: Accessible by boat

Coordinates: 45°52'18.2"N 77°11'42.1"W

Opened: Original 1887, Second 1907, Current 2021 (Replica)

Automated: N/A

Deactivated: N/A

Height: 8 meters, 27 feet

Focal Height: N/A

Signal: N/A

Foghorn Signal: N/A

Visitor Access: Grounds open, tower closed

Petite Île au Marteau Lighthouse

The original Petite Île au Marteau was opened in 1915. It had been built by S. Menier and included a square dwelling with a tower in the centre, a boathouse and an oil shed. A 5th order lens supplied the light. A fog alarm building was added in 1917. In 1955 an octagonal concrete tower, built by Gulf Maritime Construction Ltd, replaced the original. The station was deactivated in 1976

Description: Octagonal concrete tower

Location: Havre-Saint-Pierre

Directions: Accessible by boat

Coordinates: 50°12'14.9"N 63°33'30.6"W

Opened: Original 1915, Current 1955

Automated: 1987

Deactivated: 1976

Height: 11.5 meters, 38 feet

Focal Height: 14 meters, 45 feet

Signal: White flash every 2.5 seconds

Foghorn signal: Blast every 40 seconds

Visitor Access: Grounds open, tower closed

Pilier de Pierre (Stone Pillar) Lighthouse

The Pilier de Pierre (Stone Pillar) Lighthouse was opened in 1843. It is a circular stone tower, designed by Charles Atherton and built by Joseph Archer. It was automated in 1960 and continues to be active.

Description: Cylindrical tower

Location: Saint-Jean-Port-Joli

Directions: Accessible by boat

Coordinates: 47°12'20.7"N 70°21'34.4"W

Opened: 1843

Automated: 1960

Deactivated: Active

Height: 12.5 meters, 41 feet

Focal Height: 25 meters, 83 feet

Signal: White flash every 6 seconds

Foghorn Signal: N/A

Visitor Access: Closed

Pointe à la Renommée (Fame Point) Lighthouse

The original Pointe à la Renommée (Fame Point) Lighthouse was opened in 1889. The work was completed by R. Cameron and involved a square tower attached to the keeper's dwelling. In 1902 a fog control building was added. In 1907 the current cast iron lighthouse replaced the original. After the site was deactivated, the tower was moved to Quebec City but moved back a few years later after local requests. It is now a tourist attraction.

Description: Red, circular cast iron tower

Location: L'Anse-à-Valleau

Directions:
From Rivière-au-Renard, head NW on QC-132 O for 18.7 km and turn right onto Chem. de la Pointe à la Renommée. After 4.2 km you will reach the site

Coordinates: 49°06'29.9"N 64°36'01.1"W

Opened: Original 1880, Current 1907

Automated: 1975

Deactivated: Active

Height: 14 meters, 49 feet

Focal Height: Not known

Signal: White flash every 10 seconds

Foghorn Signal: 4 blasts every 70 seconds

Visitor Access: Grounds open, tower open mid-June through September

Pointe à la Citrouille Lighthouse

Pointe à la Citrouille lies at a important turn in the St. Lawrence River south of Batiscan. The station was established in 1873 with a temporary lantern on a frame but it was not until 1892 that the Pointe à la Citrouille Lighthouse was built by F.A. Verrette. The current tower replaced it in the 1980s and remains active.

Description: Square skeletal mast

Location: Batiscan

Directions: From Batiscan, head SW on Rue Principale/QC-138 O toward for 4.3 km and turn left onto Chemin du Maraîcher where the site is 850 meters

Coordinates: 46°27'06.5"N 72°16'02.6"W

Opened: Original 1873, Second 1892, Current 1980s

Automated: 1949

Deactivated: Active

Height: 16 meters, 62 feet

Focal Height: 17.5 meters, 58 feet

Signal: Fixed green

Foghorn signal: N/A

Visitor Access: Grounds open, tower closed

Pointe aux Anglais Lighthouse

The Pointe aux Anglais Lighthouse was erected in 1873 on the Ottawa River. The work was completed by Joseph White. From 1907 to 1936 the lighthouse was paired with the Oka Lighthouse to form a range. The Club de Voile des Laurentides has operated the light as a private navigation since 1998.

Description: White, square concrete tower on a pier

Location: Pointe aux Anglais

Directions: Accessible by boat

Coordinates: 45°29'37.7"N 74°10'45.8"W

Opened: Original 1872, Current 1987

Automated: 1929

Deactivated: Active

Height: 6.5 meters, 25 feet

Focal Height: 11 meters, 36 feet

Signal: Red flash every 2 seconds

Foghorn signal: N/A

Visitor Access: Grounds open, tower closed

Pointe Bonaventure Lighthouse

The Pointe Bonaventure Lighthouse was originally located at Pointe Échouerie where it was erected in 1902. It was relocated to Point Bonaventure in 1907. The lighthouse was listed as a Recognized Federal Heritage Building in 1996. It was relocated to its current position in 2005.

Description: Square pyramidal wood tower

Location: Bonaventure

Directions: From QC 132, west of Bonaventure River, turn south on Chemin Plage de Beaubassin to the end of the road to find the site

Coordinates: 48°02'08.1"N 65°28'59.2"W

Opened: 1902

Automated: 1965

Deactivated: 1988

Height: 7.5 meters, 25 feet

Focal Height: Not known

Signal: White flash every 20 seconds

Foghorn Signal: N/A

Visitor Access: Grounds open, tower closed

Pointe Carleton Lighthouse

In 1919, the Pointe Carleton Lighthouse was erected to guide ships travelling past the North Shore of Quebec and Anticosti Island. A keeper's dwelling and fog alarm building were included at the station. The site was listed as a Recognized Federal Heritage Building in 1990.

Description: Octagonal concrete tower

Location: Port-Menier

Directions: Site found just off Rte de l'Île d'Anticosti on Anticosti Island at kilometre marker 116.

Coordinates: 49°43'53.3"N 62°56'33.1"W

Opened: 1919

Automated: 1970

Deactivated: Active

Height: 12 meters, 40 feet

Focal Height: 38.5 meters, 126 feet

Signal: Green flash every 6 seconds

Foghorn signal: Blast every 60 seconds

Access: Grounds open, tower closed

Pointe des Grondines Range Lights

The original Pointe des Grondines Range Lights, as well as the Grondines Upper Range Lights, were opened in 1904 to aid vessels at a river bend near Grondines. They were replaced by the current skeleton towers after 1955. They continue to be active.

Front Range (Image above)

Description: Square skeleton

Location: Grondines

Directions: Accessible by boat

Coordinates: 46°34'43.5"N 72°04'11.8"W

Opened: Original 1904, Current not known

Automated: 1955

Deactivated: Active

Height: 9 meters, 30 feet

Focal Height: 14.5 meters, 48 feet

Signal: Fixed green

Access: Grounds open, tower closed

Rear Range

Description: Trapezoidal skeleton

Location: Grondines

Directions: Accessible by boat

Coordinates: 46°35'14.9"N 72°02'26.4"W

Opened: Original 1904, Current not known

Automated: 1955

Deactivated: Active

Height: 33 meters, 108 feet

Focal Height: 39 meters, 127 feet

Signal: Fixed green

Access: Grounds open, tower closed

Pointe des Monts Lighthouse

The Pointe des Monts Lighthouse, which opened in 1830, was the second lighthouse erected along the St. Lawrence River. It was built to aid ships around Anticosti Island and Manicouagan Shoal. A proper keeper's dwelling was not added until 1911. The site was deactivated in 1972 and the keeper's dwellings are now available for rent.

Description: Conical, white, stone tower

Location: Baie-Trinitè

Directions: From Baie-Trinité, head SW on QC-138 O for 5.2 km and turn left onto Chem. de la Pointe des Monts. and the site is 12.4 km.

Coordinates: 9°19'32.6"N 67°22'01.0"W

Opened: 1830

Automated: 1985

Deactivated: 2000

Height: 27.5 meters, 95 feet

Focal Height: 29 meters, 90 feet

Signal: White flash every 5 seconds

Foghorn: Fog cannon added in 1867

Visitor Access: Grounds open; tower open early June to mid September

Pointe du Lac Range Lights

The Pointe du Lac Range Lights opened in 1906 to guide vessels travelling the shipping channel from Nicolet Traverse to Yamachiche Bend. Skeleton towers replaced the originals and they continue to be active.

Front Range

Description: Short skeletal tower

Location: Trois-Rivières

Directions: Accessible by boat

Coordinates: 46°16'46.3"N 72°40'15.6"W

Opened: Original 1906, Current Not known

Automated: Not known

Deactivated: Active

Height: 12.5 meters, 41 feet

Focal Height: 12.5 meters, 41 feet

Signal: Fixed green

Foghorn signal: N/A

Access: Grounds open, tower closed

Rear Range (Image above)

Description: Square skeletal tower

Location: Trois-Rivières

Directions: Accessible by boat

Coordinates: 46°16'05.5"N 72°41'43.3"W

Opened: Original 1906, Current Not known

Automated: Not known

Deactivated: Active

Height: 34 meters, 112 feet

Focal Height: 49 meters, 161 feet

Signal: Fixed green

Foghorn signal: N/A

Access: Grounds open, tower closed

Pointe du Sud-Ouest Lighthouse

Request were made for a lighthouse on Anticosti Island where many ships were wrecked on its dangerous reefs. The Pointe du Sud-Ouest Lighthouse opened in 1831, the first station on the island. W. Lander oversaw the construction of the large limestone tower with keeper's dwelling enclosed. The tower was hit by fire in 1958 and a replacement tower opened in 1959. At that time the station was automated. The current skeleton tower opened in 1972 and remains active.

Description: Square skeleton tower

Location: Port-Menier

Directions: From Satellite, head NW on an unnamed road for 3.8 km and turn left on an unnamed road. After 4.3 km, turn left on an unnamed road and the site is 14.2 km

Coordinates: 49°23'29.1"N 63°35'40.9"W

Opened: Original 1831, Second 1959, Current 1972

Automated: 1959

Deactivated: Current

Height: 15 meters, 50 feet

Focal Height: 21 meters, 68 feet

Signal: White flash every 6 seconds

Foghorn Signal: N/A

Access: Grounds open, tower closed

Pointe Duthie Lighthouse

The Pointe Duthie Lighthouse opened in 1903 to mark the entrance to the Grand Cascapeida River. However it was only operational for a short time, closing in 1914. It was dismantled and moved to the British Heritage Centre in 1989. The British Heritage Centre closed in 2017 but the site can still be visited.

Description: White square pyramidal wood tower

Location: New Richmond

Directions: From New Richmond, head NW on Bd Perron O for 1.9 km and turn left on an unnamed road where the site is 1.3 km

Coordinates: 48°10'11.1"N 65°53'56.3"W

Opened: 1909

Automated: N/A

Deactivated: 1914

Height: 10 meters, 33 feet

Focal Height: 15 meters, 50 feet

Signal: Fixed white

Foghorn signal: N/A

Access: Grounds open, tower closed

Pointe Mitis Lighthouse

A lighthouse was proposed for Pointe Mitis as early as 1860 but it was not until 1874 till the Pointe Mitis Lighthouse was erected. The contract to build it was fulfilled by R. Cameron. In 1909 the current lighthouse replaced the original with the Steel Concrete Company of Montreal doing the work. A fog alarm building was added to the site in 1917. The light is currently continued by the Municipality of Métis-sur-Mer.

Description: Hexagonal cylindrical concrete tower

Location: Mètis-sur-Mer

Directions: From Métis-sur-Mer, head west on QC-132 O for 2.0 km and turn right onto Rte du Phare. After 1.0 km find the site.

Coordinates: 48°40'49.2"N 68°02'02.7"W

Opened: Original 1874, Current 1909

Automated: 1972

Deactivated: Active

Height: 21 meters, 69 feet

Focal Height: 21 meters, 69 feet

Signal: 3 white flashes every 7.5 seconds

Foghorn Signal: 3 blasts every 60 seconds

Visitor Access: Closed

Pointe Noire Range Lights

The Pointe Noire Range Lights were opened in 1875 to guide vessels to the entrance to the Saguenay River. The front tower was destroyed in an 1877 fire but was soon replaced. The lights were deactivated in 1880 but reactivated in 1903. Steel towers replaced the originals in 1952 and the current skeleton towers replaced those in 1997. They remain active.

Front Range (Image above)

Description: Square skeletal mast

Location: Baie-Sainte-Catherine

Directions: From Baie-Sainte-Catherine, head NW on QC-138 E for 2.2 km and the site

Coordinates: 48°07'23.9"N 69°43'00.5"W

Opened: Original 1875, Current 1997

Automated: 1981

Deactivated: Active

Height: 11.5 meters, 37 feet

Focal Height: 29 meters, 95 feet

Signal: Fixed white

Access: Grounds open, tower closed

Rear Range

Description: Square skeletal mast

Location: Baie-Sainte-Catherine

Directions: From Baie-Sainte-Catherine, head NW on QC-138 E for 2.6 km and the site

Coordinates: 48°07'23.9"N 69°43'00.5"W

Opened: Original 1875, Current 1997

Automated: 1981

Deactivated: Active

Height: 9 meters, 30 feet

Focal Height: 43.5 meters, 143 feet

Signal: Fixed white

Access: Grounds open, tower closed

Pointe-au-Père (Father Point) Lighthouse

The Pointe-au-Père (Father Point) Lighthouse was opened in 1909. It is a beautiful 16 sided concrete tower with 8 flying buttresses. In 1914 the worst maritime disaster in Canadian history occurred when the Empress of Ireland was struck broadside by another ship in foggy weather. 1,012 people died in the disaster. The lighting equipment was a 3rd order Fresnel lens. The site was listed as a National Historic Site of Canada in 1974.

Description: 16-sided cylindrical concrete tower with eight pyramidal buttresses

Location: Rimouski

Directions: From Rimouski, head NE on Rte 132 E/QC-132 E for 5.8 km and turn left onto Av. du Père Nouvel. After 1.0 km you will find the site

Coordinates: 48°31'01.9"N 68°28'08.0"W

Opened: 1909

Automated: 1975

Deactivated: 1975

Height: 33 meters, 108 feet

Focal Height: Not known

Signal: 4 flashes every 7.5 seconds

Foghorn signal: Fog alarm building built in 1902

Visitor Access: Grounds open, tower open early June through mid-October

Port Saint-François Range Lights

The first Port Saint-François Lighthouse opened in 1849 to guide ships into Port St. Francis harbour. In 1860 another tower was built to form the Port Saint-François Range Lights. The rear light was destroyed in a 1901 gale and a skeleton tower replaced it in 1902. In 1906 the current towers were opened, with the contract completed by Goold, Shapley & Muir. The signal was changed to fixed green at this time.

Front Range

Description: Octagonal tower on pier

Location: Port-Saint-François

Directions: Accessible by boat

Coordinates: 46°16'16.2"N 72°37'09.7"W

Opened: Original 1849, Current 1906

Automated: 1906

Deactivated: Active

Height: 11 meters, 36 feet

Focal Height: 11 meters, 36 feet

Signal: Fixed green

Access: Grounds open, tower closed

Rear Range (Image above)

Description: Trapezoidal skeleton tower

Location: Port-Saint-François

Directions: In Port-Saint-François, head NW on Rue Duval off of Chem. du Fleuve O for 80 meters and find the site

Coordinates: 46°16'16.2"N 72°37'09.7"W

Opened: Original 1860s, Current 1906

Automated: 1906

Deactivated: Active

Height: 13 meters, 43 feet

Focal Height: 19 meters, 62 feet

Signal: Fixed green

Access: Grounds open, tower closed

Portneuf Range Lights

The Portneuf Range Lights were opened in 1842 to guide vessels travelling the Richelieu Channel to Portneuf. In the 1980s they were replaced by skeleton towers. They remain active.

Front Range

Description: Skeleton Mast

Location: Portneuf

Directions: From Portneuf, head east on for 300 meters and turn left onto Rue Chem. Neuf and right on Avenue 1 and the site site

Coordinates: 46°41'40.0"N 71°51'59.3"W

Opened: Original 1842, Current 1980s

Automated: 1980s

Deactivated: Active

Height: 19 meters, 62 feet

Focal Height: 20 meters, 66 feet

Signal: Fixed green

Visitor Access: Closed

Rear Range (Image above)

Description: Skeleton Mast

Location: Portneuf

Directions: From Portneuf, head east on QC-138 E for 300 meters and turn left onto Rue Chem. Neuf and then right onto Avenue 1 for 700 meters and the site

Coordinates: 46°41'40.0"N 71°51'59.3"W

Opened: Original 1842, Current 1980s

Automated: 1980s

Deactivated: Active

Height: 13.5 meters, 47 feet

Focal Height: 41 meters, 134 feet

Signal: Fixed green

Access: Grounds open, tower closed

Pot à l'Eau-de-Vie (Brandy Pot) Lighthouse

The original Pot à l'Eau-de-Vie (Brandy Pot) Lighthouse opened in 1862 to mark the Pot a l'Eau-de-Vieu Archipelago in the St. Lawrence River. It is listed as a Recognized Federal Heritage Building. The current skeleton tower replaced the original in 1975 and continues to be active.

Description: Square skeleton tower

Location: Rivière-du-Loup

Directions: Accessible by boat

Coordinates: 47°52'20.5"N 69°40'52.7"W

Opened: Original 1862, Current 1975

Automated: 1964

Deactivated: Active

Height: 12.5 meters, 41 feet

Focal Height: 36 meters, 119 feet

Signal: Yellow flash every 2 seconds

Foghorn Signal: N/A

Access: Grounds open, tower open

Rivière du Loup Lighthouse

The Rivière du Loup Lighthouse opened in 1882 when a square wooden building with a light was erected at the end of the Rivière-du-Loup pier. The contract for the light was fulfilled by James Sheridan. In 1930 the light was moved to a nearby shed. In 1954 a skeleton tower replaced it, showing a flashing green signal.

Description: Square mast

Location: Rivière du Loup

Directions: In Rivière-du-Loup, head SW on for 1,5 km and turn right onto Rue du Quai/Rue Hayward and the light is at the end of the pier

Coordinates: 47°50'52.4"N 69°34'14.0"W

Opened: Original 1882, Second 1930, Current 1976

Automated: 1976

Deactivated: Active

Height: 8 meters, 26 feet

Focal Height: 10 meters, 33 feet

Signal: Green flash every 2 seconds

Foghorn signal: N/A

Visitor Access: Closed

Rivière Valin Range Lights

In 1873 the Canadian government built 5 pairs of range lights to guide ships travelling along the upper portion of the Saguenay River below the City of Saguenay (formerly Chicoutimi). Among them was the Rivière Valin Range Lights. In 1908 that range was replaced with a wooden front tower and a skeleton rear. Around 1977 both towers were replaced by the current skeleton towers.

Front Range (Image above)

Description: Square pyramidal skeleton

Location: Saint-Fulgence

Directions: From Saint-Fulgence, head NW on QC-172 W for 4.8 km and the site is on the right

Coordinates: 48°27'36.9"N 70°58'53.4"W

Opened: Original 1873, Current 1977

Automated: 1977

Deactivated: Active

Height: 26 meters, 85 feet

Focal Height: 27.5 meters, 90 feet

Signal: Fixed white

Visitor Access: Closed

Rear Range

Description: Square pyramidal skeleton

Location: Saint-Fulgence

Directions: From Saint-Fulgence, head NW on QC-172 W for 5.2 km and turn right on an unnamed road and the site is 330 meters

Coordinates: 48°27'36.9"N 70°58'53.4"W

Opened: Original 1893, Current 1908

Automated: 1977

Deactivated: Not known

Height: 6 meters, 20 feet

Focal Height: Not known

Signal: Fixed white

Visitor Access: Closed

Route de Contrecoeur Range Lights

In 1903, the Contrecoeur Channel was dredged between Lanoraie and Île Bouchard. Later that year three sets of range lights were opened to aid ships travelling this channel including the Route de Contrecoeur Range Lights. The original front range was a square wooden tower while the back range was a square skeleton tower. The current skeleton towers were erected some time after 1955 and continue to be active.

Front Range

Description: Square skeletal mast

Location: Contrecoeur

Directions: From Sorel-Tracy, head west on Rte Marie-Victorin/QC-132 O for 15.0 km and the site is on the right

Coordinates: 45°55'19.6"N 73°12'33.6"W

Opened: Original 1903, Current not known

Automated: Not known

Deactivated: Active

Height: 17.5 meters, 57 feet

Focal Height: 26 meters, 85 feet

Signal: Fixed yellow

Visitor Access: Closed

Rear Range (Image above)

Description: Square skeletal tower

Location: Contrecoeur

Directions: From Sorel-Tracy, head west on Rte Marie-Victorin/QC-132 O for 14.3 km and the site is on the left

Coordinates: 45°55'40.8"N 73°12'14.3"W

Opened: Current not known

Automated: Not known

Deactivated: Active

Height: 25 meters, 82 feet

Focal Height: 42 meters, 138 feet

Signal: Fixed yellow

Visitor Access: Closed

Route Île Saint-Ours Range Lights

In 1903, the Contrecoeur Channel was dredged between Lanoraie and Île Bouchard. Later that year three sets of range lights were opened to aid ships travelling this channel including the Route Île Saint-Ours Range Lights The original front range was a square wooden tower while the back range was a square skeleton tower. The current skeleton towers were erected some time after 1955 and continue to be active.

Front Range

Description: Skeleton tower

Location: Contrecoeur

Directions: Head south on Autoroute 30 O for 11.2 km and take exit 126 and after 500 turn right onto Mnt Saint-Roch. After 1.5 km turn left at the 1st cross street and the site is 3,.9 km

Coordinates: 45°53'05.4"N 73°12'57.9"W

Opened: Original 1903, Current Not known

Deactivated: Active

Height: 13 meters, 43 feet

Focal Height: 17 meters, 56 feet

Signal: Fixed green

Visitor Access: Closed

Rear Range (Image above)

Description: Skeleton tower

Location: Contrecoeur

Directions: Head south on Autoroute 30 O for 11.2 km and take exit 126 and after 500meters meters turn right onto Mnt Saint-Roch. After 1.5 km turn left at the 1st cross street and the site is 4.5 km

Coordinates: 45°52'43.7"N 73°12'59.2"W

Opened: Original 1903, Current Not known

Deactivated: Active

Height: 13 meters, 43 feet

Focal Height: 17 meters, 56 feet

Signal: Fixed green

Visitor Access: Closed

Route Louiseville Downstream Lights

The St. Lawrence River widens to form lakes in several areas such as Lake Saint-Peter. In 1906 two sets of Range Lights, Route Louisville Downstream Lights and the Route Louisville Upstream Lights, were opened to aid vessels at a turning point on the lake known as Curve No. 2. The 2 ranges had a middle tower which was common to both. The lights remain active.

Front Range (Image above)

Description: Red and white cylindrical tower

Location: Maskinongé

Directions: Accessible by boat

Coordinates: 46°11'10.5"N 72°54'58.1"W

Opened: 1906

Automated: Not known

Deactivated: Active

Height: 4 meters, 13 feet

Focal Height: 10.5 meters, 34 feet

Signal: Fixed green

Foghorn signal: N/A

Access: Grounds open, tower closed

Rear Range

Description: White cylindrical tower

Location: Maskinongé

Directions: Accessible by boat

Coordinates: 46°11'00.3"N 72°55'38.1"W

Opened: 1906

Automated: Not known

Deactivated: Active

Height: 4.5 meters, 15 feet

Focal Height: 11 meters, 36 feet

Signal: Fixed green

Foghorn signal: N/A

Access: Grounds open, tower closed

Route Louisville Upstream Lights

The St. Lawrence River widens to form lakes in several areas such as Lake Saint-Peter. In 1906 two sets of Range Lights, Route Louisville Downstream Lights and the Route Louisville Upstream Lights, were opened to aid vessels at a turning point on the lake known as Curve No. 2. The 2 ranges had a middle tower which was common to both. The lights remain active.

Front Range

Description: Orange rectangular tower

Location: Maskinongé

Directions: Accessible by boat

Coordinates: 46°11'55.6"N 72°53'24.1"W

Opened: 1906

Automated: Not known

Deactivated: Active

Height: 5 meters, 16 feet

Focal Height: 11.5 meters, 37 feet

Signal: Fixed green

Foghorn signal: N/A

Access: Grounds open, tower closed

Rear Range (Image above)

Description: White cylindrical tower

Location: Maskinongé

Directions: Accessible by boat

Coordinates: 46°11'41.4"N 72°53'43.8"W

Opened: 1906

Automated: Not known

Deactivated: Active

Height: 15 meters, 49 feet

Focal Height: 21 meters, 69 feet

Signal: Fixed green

Foghorn signal: N/A

Access: Grounds open, tower closed

Saint-Antoine Course Range Lights

In 1902 near Saint-Antoine-de-Tilly, two new sets of Range Lights were opened to guide ships along this stretch of the St. Lawrence River, the Saint-Antoine Course Range Lights and the St. Antoine Traverse Range Lights. This only involved three new towers as the middle tower served as Saint-Antoine Traverse Range Front and the Saint-Antoine Course Range Rear. The Saint-Antoine Course Range Rear range has been replaced by a skeleton tower. This range remains active

Front Range

Rear Range (Image above)

Description: Square pyramidal wood

Description: Square skeleton

Location: Saint-Antoine-de-Tilly

Location: Saint-Antoine-de-Tilly

Directions: Head northeast on Chem. de Tilly off Rte 132 for 350 meters and turn left onto Rue des Phares. After 500 meters turn right onto Pl. des Phares, the site is 100 meters

Directions: Head northeast on Chem. de Tilly off Rte 132 for 350 meters and turn left onto Rue des Phares. After 500 meters turn right onto Pl. des Phares and the site

Coordinates: 46°40'00.4"N 71°34'51.1"W

Coordinates: 46°39'58.0"N 71°35'02.8"W

Opened: 1902

Opened: Not known

Deactivated: Active

Deactivated: Active

Height: 9 meters, 30 feet

Height: 16 meters, 52 feet

Focal Height: 10 meters, 33 feet

Focal Height: 10 meters, 33 feet

Signal: Fixed green

Signal: Fixed green

Visitor Access: Closed

Visitor Access: Closed

Saint-Antoine Travese Range Lights

In 1902 near Saint-Antoine-de-Tilly, two new sets of Range Lights were opened to guide ships along this stretch of the St. Lawrence River, the Saint-Antoine Course Range Lights and the St. Antoine Traverse Range Lights. This only involved three new towers as the middle tower served as Saint-Antoine Traverse Range Front and the Saint-Antoine Course Range Rear. The Saint-Antoine Traverse Range Rear is inactive while the front remains live.

Front Range

Description: Square skeleton

Location: Saint-Antoine-de-Tilly

Directions: Head northeast on Chem. de Tilly off Rte 132 for 350 meters and turn left onto Rue des Phares. After 500 meters turn right onto Pl. des Phares, the site is 100 meters

Coordinates: 46°40'00.4"N 71°34'51.1"W

Opened: 1902

Deactivated: Active

Height: 9 meters, 30 feet

Focal Height: 10 meters, 33 feet

Signal: Fixed green

Visitor Access: Closed

Rear Range (Image above)

Description: Square skeleton

Location: Saint-Antoine-de-Tilly

Directions: Head north on Chem. de Tilly for 350 meters and turn left onto Rue des Phares and the site

Coordinates: 46°39'53.4"N 71°35'01.5"W

Opened: 1902

Deactivated: 1993

Height: 3.5 meters, 12 feet

Focal Height: N/A

Signal: Fixed green

Visitor Access: Closed

Sainte-Anne de Beaupré Lighthouse

The original Sainte-Anne de Beaupré Lighthouse was a lantern on a mast which was opened in 1888. A skeleton tower was erected about 2011 showing a sector signal and it continues to be active.

Description: Skeleton mast

Location: Sainte-Anne de Beaupré

Directions: In Sainte-Anne-de-Beaupré, head SW on Rue du Sanctuaire off BD Sainte-Anne for 140 meters and the site

Coordinates: 47°01'14.9"N 70°55'40.0"W

Opened: Original 1888, Current 2011

Automated: 2011

Deactivated: Active

Height: 9 meters, 41 feet

Focal Height: 11.5 meters, 38 feet

Signal: Red, white and green sector

Foghorn Signal: N/A

Access: Grounds open, tower close

Sainte-Anne-de-Sorel Range Lights

The Sainte-Anne-de-Sorel Range Lights were established in 1905 to aid ships travelling the Île de Grâce traverse channel near Sainte-Anne-de-Sorel. In 2011 the rear tower was replaced with a skeleton tower. Both lights continue to be active.

Front Range (Image above)

Description: Square pyramidal wood

Location: Sainte-Anne-de-Sorel

Directions: 13 Rue Dupont, Sainte-Anne-de-Sorel

Coordinates: 46°03'32.4"N 73°03'21.6"W

Opened: 1905

Automated: Not known

Deactivated: Active

Height: 9 meters, 30 feet

Focal Height: 12.5 meters, 41 feet

Signal: Fixed green

Visitor Access: Closed

Rear

Description: Triangular skeletal mast

Location: Sainte-Anne-de-Sorel

Directions: 556 Chem. du Chenal-du-Moine, Sainte-Anne-de-Sorel

Coordinates: 46°03'16.8"N 73°03'49.6"W

Opened: Original 1905, Current 2020

Automated: Not known

Deactivated: Active

Height: 9 meters, 30 feet

Focal Height: 31 meters, 102 feet

Signal: Fixed green

Visitor Access: Closed

Sainte-Croix Lighthouse

The original Sainte-Croix Lighthouse was a wooden tower opened in 1842 to guide ships in the Sainte-Croix area of the St. Lawrence River. In 1909 the lighting was upgraded with a 4th order lens. The current light is a skeleton tower which continues to be active.

Description: Skeleton tower

Location: Sainte-Croix

Directions: From Sainte-Croix, head NW on Rue du Bateau from Rue Principle for 850 meters and the site

Coordinates: 46°37'41.0"N 71°43'53.9"W

Opened: Original 1842, Current 1934

Automated: 1934

Deactivated: Active

Height: 12.5 meters, 41 feet

Focal Height: 14.5 meters, 48 feet

Signal: Fixed yellow

Foghorn signal: N/A

Visitor Access: Closed (Viewable from public road)

Sainte-Croix Range Lights

The Sainte-Croix Range Lights were opened in 1899 to mark the channel cut through the Ste. Croix bar between Montreal and Quebec. In 1934 the rear light was replaced with a square skeleton tower and in 1970 the front tower was replaced with a square skeleton tower. Both lights remain active.

Front Range

Description: Square skeletal mast

Location: Sainte-Croix

Directions: Sainte-Croix Est, head west on QC-132 O for 3.2 km and the site is on the right

Coordinates: 46°37'40.9"N 71°41'58.5"W

Opened: Original 1899 Current 1970

Automated: 1970

Deactivated: Active

Height: 7.5 meters, 25 feet

Focal Height: 60 meters, 197 feet

Signal: Fixed white

Visitor Access: Closed

Rear Range (Image above)

Description: Square skeletal mast

Location: Sainte-Croix

Directions: Sainte-Croix Est, head west on QC-132 O for 2.5 km and the site is on the right

Coordinates: 46°37'33.8"N 71°41'38.3"W

Opened: Original 1899 Current 1934

Automated: 1934

Deactivated: Active

Height: 716 meters, 52 feet

Focal Height: 75 meters, 246 feet

Signal: Fixed white

Visitor Access: Closed

Sainte-Pétronille Lighthouse

The original square wooden Sainte-Pétronille Lighthouse was opened in 1901 and marked Île de Orleans. The light was replaced by a skeleton tower in 1957 when the wharf was removed. The light remains active.

Description: Square skeleton tower

Location: Sainte-Pétronille

Directions: In Sainte-Pétronille, head SE on Rue du Quai from Che. Royal for 210 meters and the site.

Coordinates: 46°50'42.0"N 71°07'54.6"W

Opened: Original 1901, Current 1957

Automated: 1957

Deactivated: Active

Height: 14.5 meters, 36 feet

Focal Height: 15 meters, 49 feet

Signal: Yellow flash every 5 seconds

Foghorn signal: N/A

Access: Grounds open, tower closed

Saint-François Lighthouse

The original Saint-François Lighthouse was opened in 1912 with a square white lantern on the roof of a shed. It was replaced with the current skeleton tower sometime after 1955 and it remains active.

Description: Square skeleton tower

Location: Saint-François-de-l'Île-d'Orléans

Directions: From Saint-François-de-l'Île-d'Orléans, head SW on Chem. Royal/QC-368 E for 100 meters and turn left onto Chem. du Quai where the site is at the tip of the wharf

Coordinates: 46°59'47.6"N 70°48'29.5"W

Opened: Original 1912, Current not known

Automated: Not known

Deactivated: Active

Height: 9 meters, 30 feet

Focal Height: 11 meters 37 feet

Signal: White flash every 5 seconds

Foghorn signal: N/A

Access: Grounds open, tower closed

Saint-Laurent Lighthouse

The original Saint-Laurent Lighthouse opened in 1869 at the end of a newly constructed wharf in Saint Laurent-de-l'Île-d'Orléans. In 1902 the wharf was lengthened and the light was moved to the top of a freight shed on the wharf. In 1814 a steel skeleton tower was built on the wharf to replace it. Finally in 2011 a ferry dock was opened on the wharf and the light was attached to the docking gate, It remains active.

Description: Light mounted atop the steel frame of ferry dock

Location: Saint Laurent-de-l'Île-d'Orléans

Directions: In Saint Laurent-de-l'Île-d'Orléans, head SE on Chem. du Quai from QC-368 and the site is on the end of the wharf

Coordinates: 46°51'28.9"N 71°00'10.5"W

Opened: Original 1869, Current 2011

Automated: Not known

Deactivated: Active

Height: 12.5 meters, 21 feet

Focal Height: 14 meters, 46 feet

Signal: Green flash every 5 seconds

Foghorn Signal: N/A

Visitor Access: Access: Grounds open, tower closed

Saint-Michel Range Lights

The Saint-Michel Range Lights were opened in 1928 to aid ships travelling on the St. Lawrence River south side near Saint-Michel-de-Bellechasse. They were replaced by skeleton towers in 2006 which remain active.

Front Range

Description: Triangular skeletal mast

Location: Saint-Michel

Directions: Saint-Michel-de-Bellechasse, head NW on Rue Santerre off Rue Principal for 140 meters and the site

Coordinates: 46°52'31.0"N 70°54'59.8"W

Opened: Original 1928, Current 2006

Automated: Not known

Deactivated: Active

Height: 25 meters, 82 feet

Focal Height: 30 meters, 97 feet

Signal: Fixed white

Visitor Access: Closed

Rear Range (Image above)

Description: Square skeletal mast

Location: Saint-Michel

Directions: Saint-Michel-de-Bellechasse, head SW on QC-132 O for 1.0 km and the site is on the left

Coordinates: 46°52'31.0"N 70°54'59.8"W

Opened: Original 1928, Current 2006

Automated: Not known

Deactivated: Active

Height: 25 meters, 82 feet

Focal Height: 30 meters, 97 feet

Signal: Fixed white

Visitor Access: Closed

Saint-Siméon Lighthouse

The original Saint-Siméon Lighthouse opened in 1906 to guide ships travelling to Saint-Siméon. It was a light from an wooden lantern with a 5th order lens. It was replaced with a skeleton tower and continues to be active.

Description: Square cylindrical skeleton tower

Location: Saint-Siméon

Directions: In Saint-Siméon, head SE on Rue du Quai from Rue St Laurent for 450 meters and the light is on the end of the ferry dock

Coordinates: 47°50'23.7"N 69°52'23.0"W

Opened: Original 1906, Current Ca.1971

Automated: Not known

Deactivated: Active

Height: 8 meters, 26 feet

Focal Height: 9 meters, 30 feet

Signal: Red flash every 2 seconds

Foghorn Signal: N/A

Visitor Access: Closed

Soulanges Canal Lower Entrance Range Lights

A series of rapids obstructed ships travel on the St. Lawrence River upstream from Montreal. In 1841 the Beauharnois Canal along the south shore was opened in order to bypass them and 1899 the deeper Soulanges Canal was completed. In 1902, a set of range lights were erected, the Soulanges Canal Lower Entrance Range Lights and the Soulanges Canal Upper Entrance Range Lights. All of the lights were made inactive in 1960.

Front Range (Image above)

Description: Cast iron tower

Location: Pointe-des-Cascades

Directions: From Pointe-des-Cascades, head NE on Chem. de l'Aqueduc for 280 meters, turn left onto Rue Centrale and then right onto Chem. du Canal and the site is 1.3 km

Coordinates: 45°20'09.3"N 73°57'18.8"W

Opened: 1902

Automated: Not known

Deactivated: 1960

Height: 6.5 meters, 21.5 feet

Focal Height: 10.5 meters, 34 feet

Signal: Fixed Red

Access: Grounds open, tower closed

Rear Range

Description: Cast iron tower

Location: Pointe-des-Cascades

Directions: From Pointe-des-Cascades, head NE on Chem. de l'Aqueduc for 280 meters and turn right onto Rue Centrale. After 150 meters turn left onto Chem. du Fleuve, then left and the site

Coordinates: 45°19'51.1"N 73°58'06.4"W

Opened: 1902

Automated: Not known

Deactivated: 1960

Height: 13.5 meters, 45 feet

Focal Height: 18 meters, 59 feet

Signal: Fixed Red

Access: Grounds open, tower closed

Soulanges Upper Lower Entrance Range Lights

A series of rapids obstructed ships travel on the St. Lawrence River upstream from Montreal. In 1841 the Beauharnois Canal along the south shore was opened in order to bypass them and 1899 the deeper Soulanges Canal was completed. In 1902, a set of range lights were erected, the Soulanges Canal Lower Entrance Range Lights and the Soulanges Canal Upper Entrance Range Lights. All of the lights were made inactive in 1960.

Front Range (Image above)

Description: Cast iron tower

Location: Les Coteaux

Directions: 64 Rue Principale, Les Coteaux

Coordinates: 45°15'27.8"N 74°12'02.2"W

Opened: 1902

Automated: Not known

Deactivated: 1960

Height: 11 meters, 35 feet

Focal Height: 9.5 meters, 31 feet

Signal: Fixed Red

Access: Grounds open, tower closed

Rear Range

Description: Cast iron tower

Location: Les Coteaux

Directions: From Les Coteaux, head east on Chem. du Fleuve from QC-338 for 130 meters to the site

Coordinates: 45°15'40.4"N 74°11'48.6"W

Opened: 1902

Automated: Not known

Deactivated: 1960

Height: 11 meters, 30 feet

Focal Height: 14 meters, 46 feet

Signal: Fixed Red

Access: Grounds open, tower closed

St. Pierre Les Becquets Lighthouse

The original St. Pierre Les Becquets Lighthouse was opened in 1844 to mark the Saint-Pierre-les-Becquets wharf for the regular ferry service. At some point after 1955 the current cylindrical mast replaced it.

Description: White cylindrical mast

Location: Saint-Pierre-Les-Becquets

Directions: Saint-Pierre-Les-Becquets, head north on QC-132 E for 1.0 km and take a left onto Chem. du Quai and the site

Coordinates: 46°30'27.1"N 72°12'21.5"W

Opened: Original 1844, Current

Automated: Not known

Deactivated: Not known

Height: 6.5 meters, 26 feet

Focal Height: 8 meters

Signal: Fixed green

Foghorn signal: N/A

Access: Grounds open, tower closed

Tétreauville Range Lights

The original Tétreauville Range Lights were opened in Montreal in 1911 to mark the ship channel from Ile aux Vaches Traverse to Longue Pointe Curve. The front range was a square wooden lantern rising from a square, wooden building while the rear range was a steel skeleton tower. A circular metal tower replaced the front range Ca.1971 and a circular metal tower replaced the rear range sometime after 1971. They remain active.

Front Range (Image above)

Description: Steel post with daymark

Location: Montreal

Directions: In Montreal, head NW on Rue de Beaurivage from Rue Notre Dame for 600 meters and turn right onto Rue Ontario E. After 80 meters turn right onto Pl. Arthur and the site

Coordinates: 45°35'32.1"N 73°30'49.9"W

Opened: Original 1911, Current not known

Deactivated: Active

Height: 7.5 meters, 25 feet

Focal Height: 24.5 meters, 48 feet

Signal: Fixed green

Access: Grounds open, tower closed

Rear Range

Description: Steel post with daymark

Location: Montreal

Directions: In Montreal, head east on Rue Mousseau off Rue Notre Dame for 130 meters and turn right onto Rue Bellerive and the site

Coordinates: 45°35'50.6"N 73°30'37.9"W

Opened: Original 1911, Current not known

Deactivated: Active

Height: 22 meters, 72 feet

Focal Height: 30 meters, 98 feet

Signal: Fixed green

Access: Grounds open, tower closed

Traverse Cap-Santé Range Lights

The original Traverse Cap-Santé Range Lights opened in 1842 to aid vessels travelling upstream on the St. Lawrence River from Portnuef. At some point after 1955 these original wooden towers were replaced with a circular steel tower for the front range and a skeleton tower for the rear range. These lights remain active.

Front Range (Image above)

Description: Skeleton mast

Location: Portneuf

Directions: From Portneuf, head SW on an unnamed road from QC-138 for 90 meters and the site is 100 meters south

Coordinates: 46°41'23.8"N 71°52'35.3"W

Opened: Original 1842, Current not known

Automated: Not known

Deactivated: Active

Height: 19 meters, 62 feet

Focal Height: 30 meters, 66 feet

Signal: Fixed green

Visitor Access: Closed

Rear Range

Description: Skeleton mast

Location: Portneuf

Directions: In Portnuef, off QC-138 between Rue Ableson and Rue de la Dreve

Coordinates: 46°41'32.8"N 71°53'00.4"W

Opened: Original 1842, Current not known

Automated: Not known

Deactivated: Active

Height: 14.5 meters, 47 feet

Focal Height: 31 meters, 134 feet

Signal: Fixed green

Visitor Access: Closed

Traverse Longue-Pointe Range Lights

The original Traverse Longue-Pointe Range Lights were opened in 1903 to aid ships travelling on the St. Lawrence River at Longue-Pointe. They consisted of lanterns on poles. In 1904 they were replaced by wooden towers in a contract fulfilled by J.B. Laflamme and J.G. Howard. They were replaced in turn by cylindrical metal towers sometime after 1977 and remain active.

Front Range

Description: Cylindrical metal tower

Location: Longueuil

Directions: In Longueuil, head southwest on QC-132 O off Route Transcanadienne for 2.3 km and the site is on the right

Coordinates: 45°33'42.5"N 73°29'41.0"W

Opened: Original 1903, Current Not known

Automated: Not known

Deactivated: Active

Height: 12 meters, 39 feet

Focal Height: Not known

Signal: Fixed red

Access: Grounds open, tower closed

Rear Range (Image above)

Description: Cylindrical metal tower

Location: Longueuil

Directions: From Verchères, head northeast on QC-132 E for 3.5 km and the site is on the right

Coordinates: 45°47'55.1"N 73°19'19.6"W

Opened: Original 1903, Current Not known

Automated: Not known

Deactivated: Active

Height: 13.5 meters, 44 feet

Focal Height: Not known

Signal: Fixed red

Access: Grounds open, tower closed

Verchères Traverse Range Lights

The original Verchères Traverse Range Lights opened in 1903 to mark the channel between Verchères and Contrecoeur. The front light was a wooden tower and the back light was on the tower of an old windmill. The current cylindrical tower of the front range was opened in 1967 and a similar tower was opened for the back range in 1972. They remain active.

Front Range (Image above)

Description: Post with orange daymark

Location: Verchères

Directions: From Verchères, head northeast on QC-132 E for 3.0 km and the site is on the right

Coordinates: 45°47'55.1"N 73°19'19.6"W

Opened: Original 1902, Current 1967

Automated: Not known

Deactivated: Active

Height: 12.5 meters, 41 feet

Focal Height: 16 meters, 52 feet

Signal: Fixed green

Access: Grounds open, tower closed

Rear Range

Description: Square skeleton mast

Location: Verchères

Directions: From Verchères, head northeast on QC-132 E for 2.5 km and the site is on the left:

Coordinates: 45°47'46.2"N 73°19'38.6"W

Opened: Original 1902, Current 1972

Automated: Not known

Deactivated: Active

Height: 16 meters, 52 feet

Focal Height: 25 meters, 82 feet

Signal: Fixed green

Access: Grounds open, tower closed

Verchères Village Range Lights

The original Verchères Village Range Lights were opened in 1902 to mark a new dredged channel between Île Bouchard and the south shore of the St. Lawrence River. This consisted of two wooden towers. The front tower was replaced by a skeleton tower in 1929. The lights remain active.

Front Range (Image above)

Description: Square skeleton tower

Location: Verchères

Directions: In Verchères , head north on Rue Saint-Laurent from Rte Marie-Victorin for meters to find the site

Coordinates: 45°46'46.0"N 73°21'22.4"W

Opened: Original 1902, Current 1929

Automated: Not known

Deactivated: Active

Height: 6 meters, 20 feet

Focal Height: 9.5 meters, 32 feet

Signal: Fixed green

Access: Grounds open, tower closed

Rear Range

Description: Square skeleton tower

Location: Verchères

Directions: In Verchères , head NW on Rue de l'Aqueduc off Rte 132 for see the site to 85 your left

Coordinates: 45°46'30.3"N 73°21'41.4"W

Opened: 1902

Automated: Not known

Deactivated: Active

Height: 24.5 meters, 80 feet

Focal Height: 31 meters, 102 feet

Signal: Fixed green

Access: Closed

Other Lighthouses1

Name: Bouchard Range
Opened: 1914
Coordinates: 45°48'59.1"N 73°20'50.7"W

Location: Saint-Sulpice
Access: Grounds open, tower closed

Name: Cap-aux-Corbeaux Range
Opened: 1915
Coordinates: 47°26'06.7"N 70°25'40.7"W

Location: Cap-aux-Corbeaux
Access: Closed

Name: Cap-de-la-Madeleine Wharf Range
Opened: 1904
Coordinates: 46°21'52.8"N 72°29'54.0"W

Location: Trois-Rivières
Access: Grounds open, tower closed

Name: Champlain
Opened: Original 1844, Current not known
Coordinates: 46°26'22.7"N 72°20'41.9"W

Location: Champlain
Access: Closed

Name: Gallia Bay Lower Range
Opened: 1907
Coordinates: 46°05'42.0"N 73°00'12.5"W

Location: Sorel-Tracy
Access: Grounds open, tower closed

Name: Gallia Bay Upper Range
Opened: 1907
Coordinates: 46°05'24.6"N 73°00'41.5"W

Location: Sorel-Tracy
Access: Grounds open, tower closed

Name: Grande Île Kamouraska
Opened: Original 1862, Current 1982
Coordinates: 47°37'20.4"N 69°51'44.3"W

Location: Kamouraska
Access: Grounds open, tower closed

Name: Île aux Vaches Traverse Range
Opened: 1902
Coordinates: 45°41'12.6"N 73°26'33.1"W

Location: Varennes
Access: Grounds open, tower closed

Name: Île de Bellechasse
Opened: Original 1862, Current 1969
Coordinates: 46°55'53.5"N 70°46'02.6"W

Location: Berthier-sur-Mer
Access: Grounds open, tower closed

Name: Île Deslauriers Range
Opened: 1902
Coordinates: 45°41'36.4"N 73°27'37.9"W

Location: Varennes
Access: Closed

Other Lighthouses2

Name: Île Joncas
Opened: 1906
Coordinates: 50°10'56.9"N 61°50'38.9"W

Location: Natashquan
Access: Grounds open, tower closed

Name: Île Ste-Thérèse Lower Range
Opened: 1871
Coordinates: 45°41'06.7"N 73°27'32.8"W

Location: Rareness
Access: Grounds open, tower closed

Name: Lavaltrie Range Lights
Opened: Original 1831, Current 1915
Coordinates: 45°52'59.1"N 73°15'50.1"W

Location: Lavaltrie
Access: Grounds open, tower closed

Name: Lower Allumette Lake
Opened: Original 1885, Current 1910
Coordinates: 45°51'26.3"N 76°56'03.0"W

Location: Chapeau
Access: Grounds open, tower closed

Name: Mousseau Range
Opened: 1914
Coordinates: 45°50'13.9"N 73°18'14.5"W

Location: Saint-Sulpice
Access: Grounds open, tower closed

Name: Petite Traverse Range
Opened: 1904
Coordinates: 45°54'40.1"N 73°12'29.2"W

Location: Contrecoeur
Access: Grounds open, tower closed

Name: Pointe de l'Ouest
Opened: Original 1858, Current 1967
Coordinates: 49°51'50.6"N 64°31'23.7"W

Location: Port-Menier
Access: Grounds open, tower closed

Name: Pointe de la Prairie
Opened: Original 1931, Current 1972
Coordinates: 47°24'33.8"N 70°25'51.2"W

Location: Saint-Bernard-sur-Mer
Access: Closed

Name: Port Daniel Ouest
Opened: 1907
Coordinates: 48°09'05.3"N 64°56'58.5"W

Location: Port-Daniel
Access: Grounds open, tower closed

Name: Rimouski
Opened: 1906
Coordinates: 48°28'51.9"N 68°31'02.1"W

Location: Rimouski
Access: Grounds open, tower closed

Other Lighthouses3

Name: Rocher aux Oiseaux
Opened: 1870
Coordinates: 47°50'18.1"N 61°08'41.2"W

Location: Cap-aux-Meules
Access: Closed

Name: Saint-Jean-d'Orléans
Opened: 1874
Coordinates: 46°54'56.7"N 70°53'47.0"W

Location: Saint-Jean-de-l'Île-d'Orléans
Access: Grounds open, tower closed

Name: Traverse Contrecoeur Range
Opened: 1904
Coordinates: 45°49'55.5"N 73°16'54.2"W

Location: Contrecoeur
Access: Closed

Tours

Anticosti Island Tour

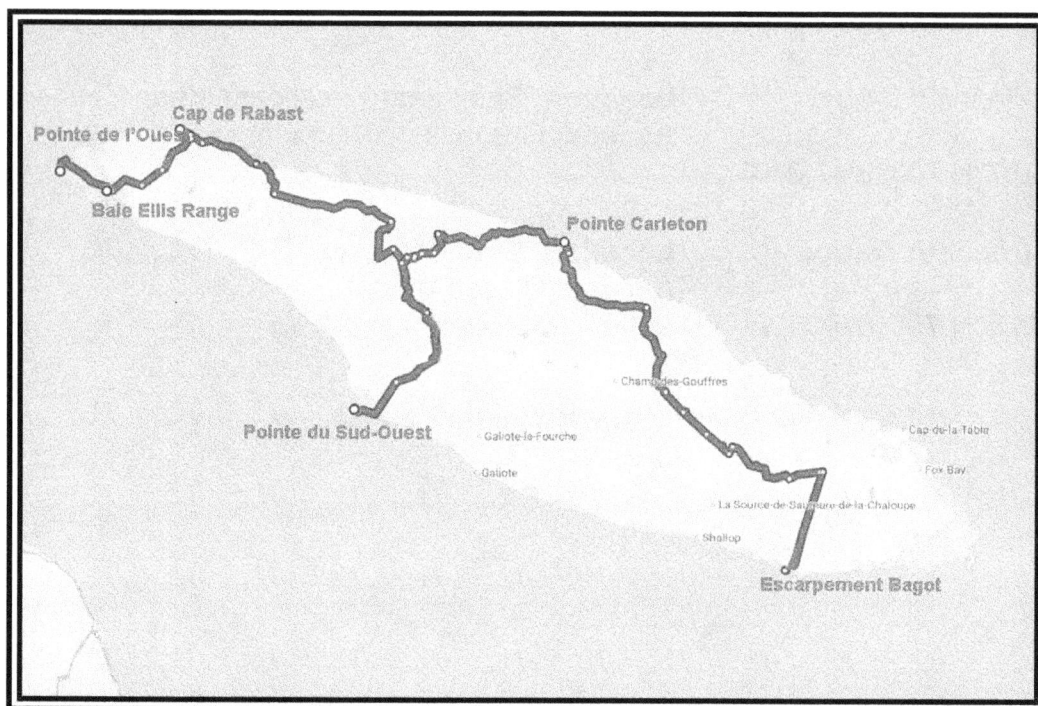

6 Lighthouses, 8 hours driving

Pointe de l'Ouest	49°51'50.6"N 64°31'23.7"W
Baie Ellis Range	49°49'30.5"N 64°22'31.3"W
Cap de Rabast	49°57'05.8"N 64°08'57.4"W
Pointe du Sud-Ouest	49°23'29.1"N 63°35'40.9"W
Pointe Carleton	49°43'53.3"N 62°56'33.1"W
Escarpement Bagot	49°03'57.9"N 62°15'35.1"W

Note that there is one more lighthouse on the island but there are no roads to it and needs to be accessed by boat

Cap de la Table	49°21'04.3"N 61°53'46.2"W

Gaspé Tour1

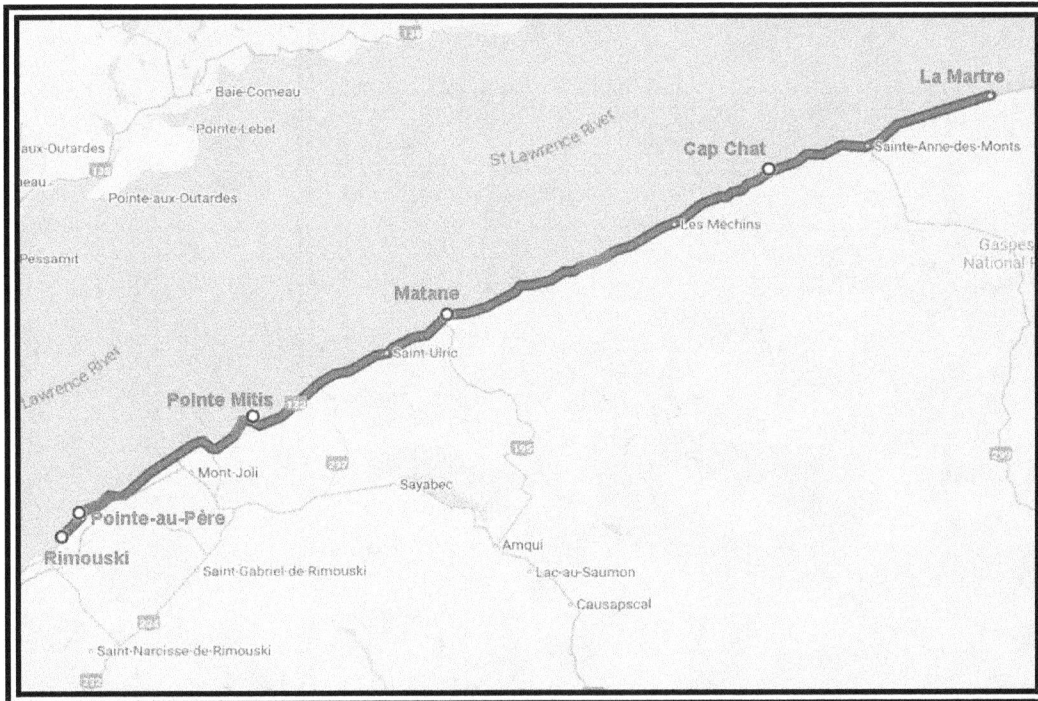

6 lighthouses, 2 hours 30 minutes

Rimouski	48°28'39.3"N 68°30'36.9"W
Pointe-au-Père	48°31'01.9"N 68°28'08.0"W
Pointe Mitis	48°40'49.2"N 68°02'02.7"W
Matane	48°50'59.8"N 67°32'57.5"W
Cap Chat	49°05'20.6"N 66°44'27.7"W
La Martre	49°12'22.1"N 66°10'16.8"W

Gaspé Tour2

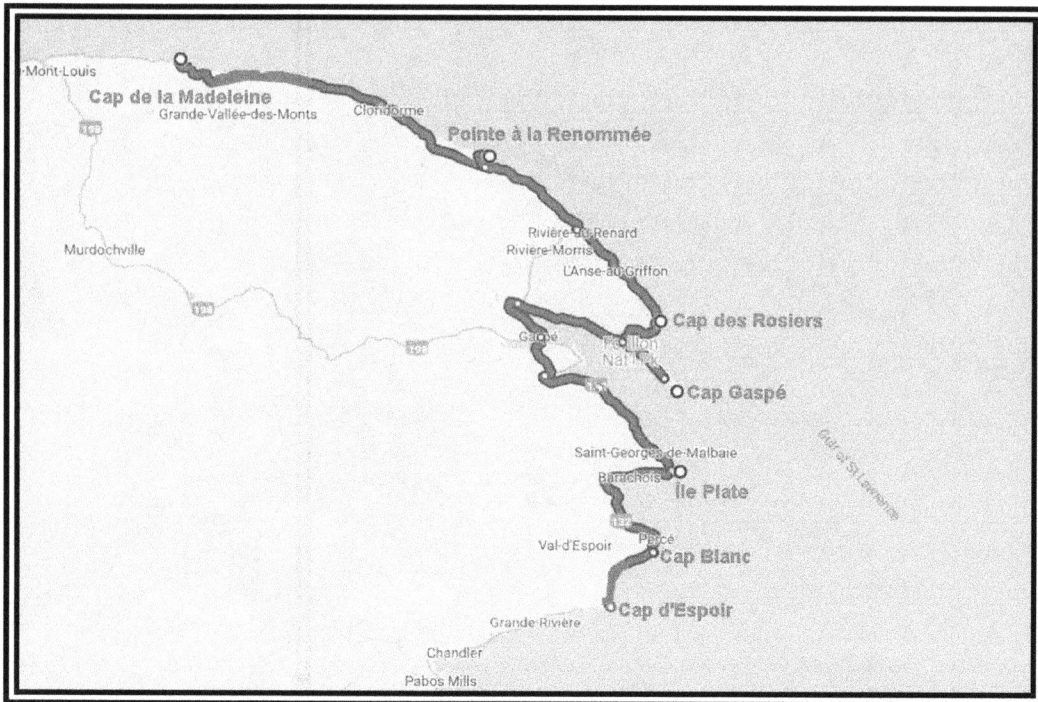

7 lighthouses, 4 hours driving

Cap de la Madeleine	49°15'04.0"N 65°19'31.1"W
Pointe à la Renommée	49°06'29.9"N 64°36'01.1"W
Cap des Rosiers	48°51'20.9"N 64°12'02.2"W
Cap Gaspé	48°44'57.0"N 64°09'49.5"W
Île Plate (Gaspé)	48°37'37.3"N 64°09'22.7"W
Cap Blanc	48°30'04.9"N 64°13'06.4"W
Cap d'Espoir	48°25'08.0"N 64°19'05.2"W

Montreal Tour

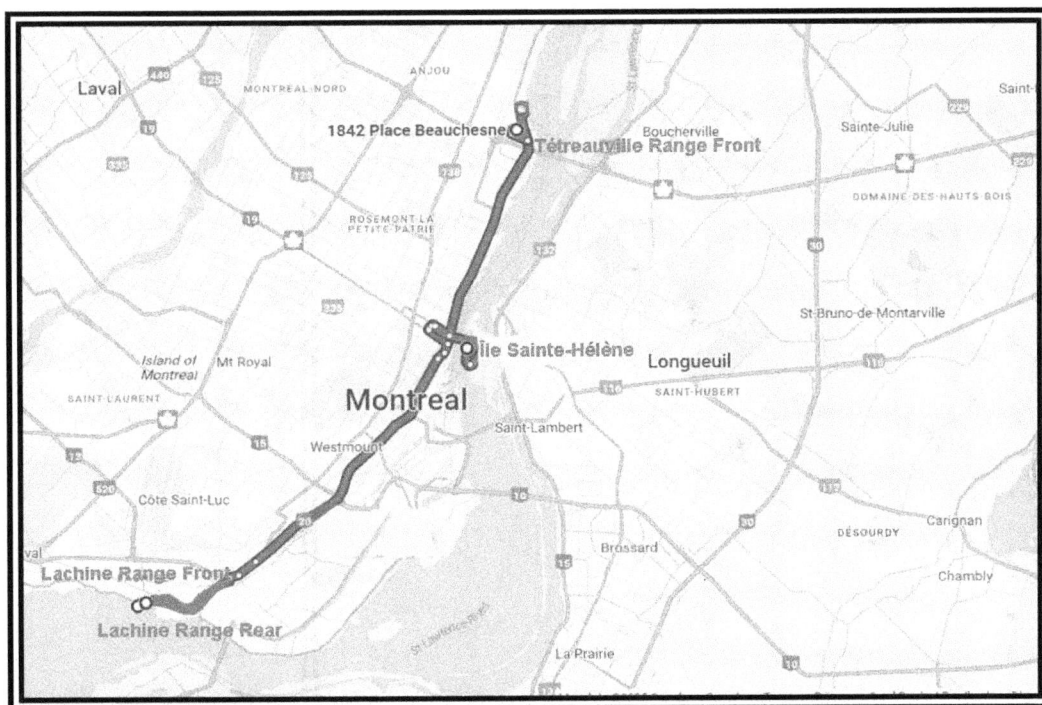

5 lighthouses, 1 hour 15 minutes driving

Lachine Range Front	45°25'56.1"N 73°41'41.7"W
Lachine Range Rear	45°25'59.5"N 73°41'28.0"W
Île Sainte-Hélène	45°31'06.9"N 73°32'17.6"W
Tétreauville Range Front	45°35'32.1"N 73°30'49.9"W
Tétreauville Range Rear	45°35'50.6"N 73°30'37.9"W

Quebec City Tour

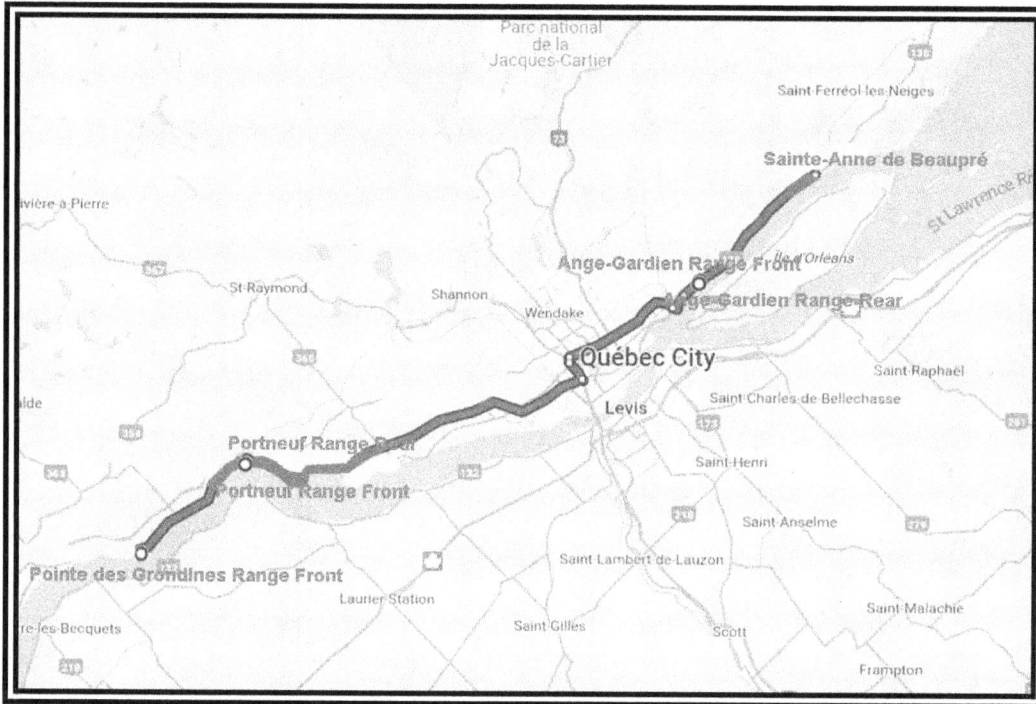

6 Lighthouses, 1 hour 30 minutes driving

Pointe des Grondines Range Front	46°35'14.9"N 72°02'26.4"W
Portneuf Range Front	46°41'22.9"N 71°52'12.8"W
Portneuf Range Rear	46°41'40.0"N 71°51'59.3"W
Ange-Gardien Range Rear	46°53'56.0"N 71°07'14.0"W
Ange-Gardien Range Front	46°54'08.2"N 71°07'06.2"W
Sainte-Anne de Beaupré	47°01'14.9"N 70°55'40.0"W

St Lawrence Range Tour

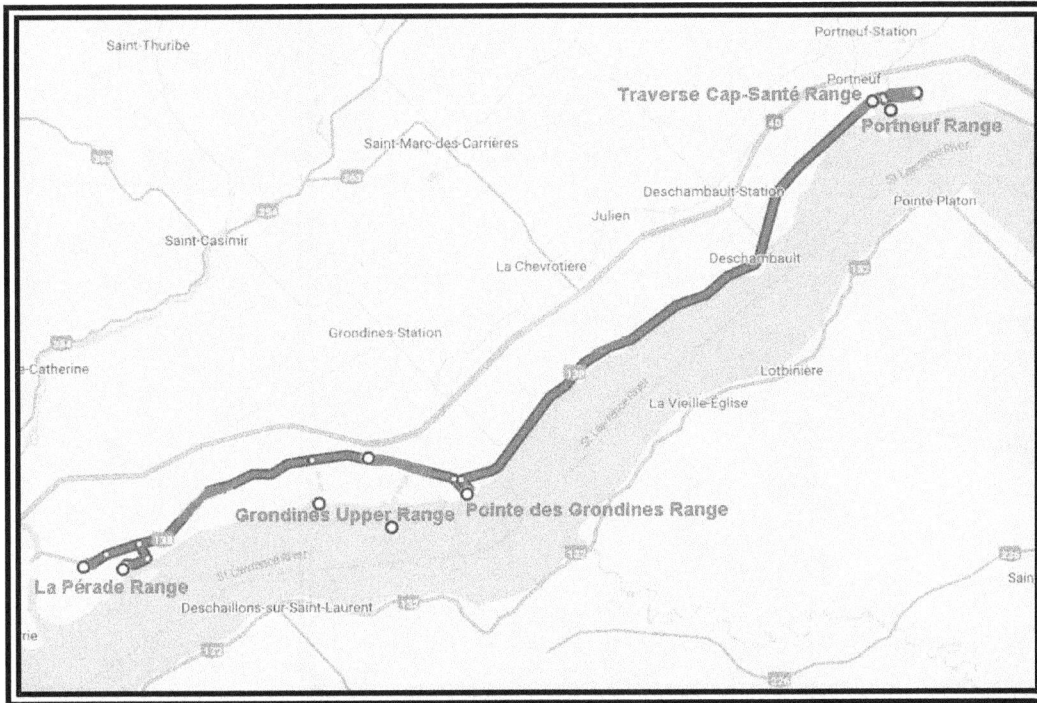

10 lighthouses, 45 minutes driving

La Pérade Range Rear	46°34'05.1"N 72°11'19.9"W
La Pérade Range Front	46°34'02.9"N 72°10'23.8"W
Grondines Upper Range Front	46°35'06.5"N 72°05'51.9"W
Grondines Upper Range Rear	46°35'49.9"N 72°04'43.4"W
Pointe des Grondines Range Rear	46°34'43.5"N 72°04'11.8"W
Pointe des Grondines Range Front	46°35'14.9"N 72°02'26.4"W
Traverse Cap-Santé Range Front	46°41'23.8"N 71°52'35.3"W
Traverse Cap-Santé Range Rear	46°41'32.8"N 71°53'00.4"W
Portneuf Range Front	46°41'22.9"N 71°52'12.8"W
Portneuf Range Rear	46°41'40.0"N 71°51'59.3"W

Trois Rivieres Tour

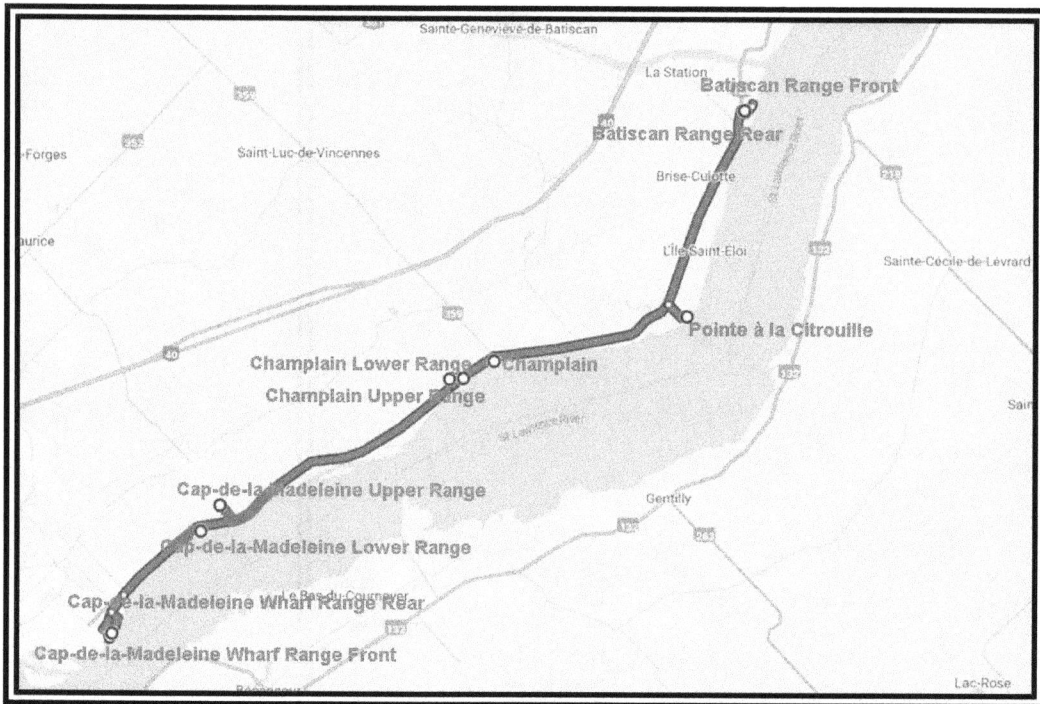

10 lighthouses, 35 minutes driving

Cap-de-la-Madeleine Wharf Range Front	46°21'52.8"N 72°29'54.0"W
Cap-de-la-Madeleine Wharf Range Rear	46°21'56.3"N 72°29'51.1"W
Cap-de-la-Madeleine Lower Range	46°23'36.2"N 72°27'44.8"W
Cap-de-la-Madeleine Upper Range	46°24'01.4"N 72°27'17.0"W
Champlain Upper Range	46°26'05.2"N 72°21'47.2"W
Champlain Lower Range	46°26'06.2"N 72°21'26.0"W
Champlain	46°26'22.7"N 72°20'41.9"W
Pointe à la Citrouille	46°27'06.5"N 72°16'02.6"W
Batiscan Range Rear	46°30'26.6"N 72°14'40.7"W
Batiscan Range Front	46°30'33.6"N 72°14'22.9"W

Glossary of Lighthouse Terms

Aerobeacon: A lighting system which creates a signal over long distances. It consists of a strong light source with a focusing mechanism which is rotated on a vertical axis. It has been used at airports as well as lighthouses.

Acetylene: After 1910, acetylene began to be used to power the lighthouse light source. It has the advantage that it could be stored on site with a sun valve turning it on at dusk and off at daybreak.

Alternating Light: A light source which changes colours in a regular pattern.

Arc of Visibility: The range of the horizon from which the lighthouse is visible from the sea.

Automated: A lighthouse that operates without a keeper. The light functions are controlled by timers, and light and fog detectors.

Beacon: A fixed aid to navigation.

Bell: A sound signal produced by fixed aids and by sea movement on buoys.

Breakwater: A structure that protects a shore area or harbour by blocking waves.

Bull's-eye Lens: A convex lens used to refract light.

Catwalk: An elevated walkway which allows the keeper to move in the lantern room in towers built in the sea.

Characteristic: The distinct pattern of the flashing light or foghorn blast which allows seamen to distinguish which light station it is coming from.

Chariot: A wheeled assembly at the bottom of a Fresnel lens which is rotated around a circular track.

Clockwork Mechanism: Early lighthouses had a series of gears, pulleys and weights, which had to be wound on a recurring basis by the keepers.

Cottage Style Lighthouse: A lighthouse made up of a keeper's residence with a light on top.

Crib: A base structure filled with stone which acted as the foundation for the structure built on top.

Daymark: A unique colour pattern that identifies a specific lighthouse during the day.

Decommissioned: A lighthouse that has discontinued operating as a aid to navigation.

Diaphone: A sound signal produced by a slotted piston moved by compressed air.

Directional Light: A light which marks the direction to be followed.

Eclipse: The interval between light flashed or foghorn blasts.

Fixed Light: A light shining continuously without periods of eclipse or darkness.

Flashing Light: A light pattern distinguished by periods of eclipse or darkness.

Focal Plane: The path of a beam of light emitted from a lighthouse. The height from the center of the beam to the sea is known as the height of the focal plane.

Fog Detector: A device used to automatically determine conditions which may reduce visibility and the need to start a sound signal.

Fog Signal: An audible device such as a bell or horn that warns seamen during period of fog when the light would be ineffective.

Fresnel Lens: An optic system composed of a convex lens and prisms which concentrate the light beam through a series of prisms. The design was produced by Augustin Fresnel in the 1800s.

Geographic Range: The longest distance the curvature of the earth allows an object of a certain height to be seen.

Isophase Light: A light in which the duration of light and darkness are equal.

Keeper: The person responsible for the maintenance and operation of the lighthouse.

Lamp and Reflector: A lamp and polished mirror used before the invention of more effective optic systems such as the Fresnel lens.

Lantern: A glass covered space at the top of the lighthouse tower, which housed the lighting equipment.

Lens: The glass optical system used to concentrate and direct the light.

Light Sector: The arc over which a light can be seen from the sea.

Lightship: A ship that served as a lighthouse.

Light Station: The lighthouse tower as well as any outbuildings such as the keeper's quarters, fog-signal building, fuel storage building and boathouse.

Nautical Mile: A unit of distance which is the average distance on the Earth's surface represented by one minute of latitude. It is equal to 1.1508 statute miles and mainly used at sea.

Nominal Range: The distance a light can be seen in good weather.

Occulting Light: A light in which the period of light is longer than the period of darkness and in which the intervals of darkness are all equal. Also known as an eclipsing light.

Order: A description of the power of the Fresnel lens ranging from one to seven from stronger to weaker.

Parabolic Reflector: A metal bowl shaped to a parabolic curve which reflects a lamp's light from it's center.

Parapet: A railed walkway which surrounds the lamp room.

Period: The total time for one cycle of the pattern of the light or sound signal.

Pharologist: A person with an interest in lighthouses.

Range Lights: Two lights which form a range provide direction to mariners for safe passage. They are described as the Front and Rear Lighthouses or the Inner and Outer. The front range light is lower than the rear, and when they align,the ship is in the proper position.

Revetment: A bank of stone laid to protect a structure against erosion from waves.

Revolving Light: A flash produced by the rotation of a Fresnel lens.

Riprap: Broken rocks or stone placed to help prevent erosion.

Sector: The portion of the sea lit by a sector light.

Skeleton Tower: Towers consisting of four or more braced feet with a beacon on top. They have little resistance to the wind and waves, and bear up well in a storm.

Solar-powered Optic: Many automated lights are run on solar powered batteries.

Spider Lamp: A brass container holding oil and solid wicks.

Tender: A ship which services lighthouses.

Ventilator: Opening' at the top of a lighthouse tower to provide heat exhaust and air flow within the tower.

Wick Solid: A solid cord which draws fuel to the flame in spider lamps.

Photo Credits

busand2003: Sainte-Madeleine-de-la-Rivière
Canada Coast Guard: Banc du Cap Brûlé Downstream Rear Range, Bécancour Front Range, Champlain Upper Rear Range, Contrecoeur-Verchères Front, Escarpement Bagot, Ile à l'Aigle Rear Range, Ile aux Oeufs, Ile aux Raisins Front, Ile Bouchard Rear, Ile de Grâce, Ile des Barques Front Range, Ile Greenly, Ile Plate, Île-RougeÎle-Rouge, Long Pèlerin, Maskinongé Curve, Passage Lower, Pointe aux Anglais, Pointe Citrouille, Pointe du Sud-Ouest, Port Saint-François Rear, Saint-Antoine Traverse Rear; **Canada Fisheries and Oceans**: Île du Grand Caouis, Île Ste-Thérèse Upper Range Front, Île-du-Grand-Caoui, Pilier-de-Pierre; **Canada Library and Archives**: Cape Dogs; **Claude Brochu**: Ile du Havre Aubert; **Danielle Langlois**: Brion Island; **Dennis Jarvis**: Cabano, Cape Blanc, Ile Du Moine Front Range, III St. Mary, Lotbiniere Front Range, Nicolet Sector, Pointe Bonaventure, Saint Anne De Sorel Front Range, Verchères Village Front Range; **Harfang**: Pointe-des-Monts; **Jeangagnon**: Lachine, Cap-d Espoir; **Laurent Bélanger**: Cap-Chat; **Nicogag**: l'île Verte; **Samuel Bouchard**: Cap Saumon; **SaphirQC**: Ile du Pot; **Stéphane Batigne**: l'île Verte; **Wladyslaw**: Prince Shoal

All other images by the author

The Photographer's and Explorer's Series

Unless noted, there are Print and eBook editions available for the following.

Birding Guide to Orkney
Guide to Photographing Birds

Maine Lighthouses
Lighthouses of British Columbia
New Brunswick Lighthouses
Newfoundland Lighthouses
Nova Scotia Lighthouses
Ontario Lighthouses
Orkney and Shetland Lighthouses (eBook)
Prince Edward Island Lighthouses
Lighthouses of Scotland

Ontario's Old Mills
Ontario Waterfalls

Alabama Covered Bridges (eBook)
Covered Bridges of Canada
California Covered Bridges (eBook)
Connecticut Covered Bridges (eBook)
Georgia Covered Bridges (eBook)
Illinois Covered Bridges
Indiana Covered Bridges
Iowa Covered Bridges
Maine Covered Bridges (eBook)
Massachusetts Covered Bridges (eBook)
Michigan Covered Bridges (eBook)
New Brunswick Covered Bridges
New England Covered Bridges
Covered Bridges of the Mid-Atlantic
Covered Bridges of the South
New Hampshire Covered Bridges
New York Covered Bridges
Ohio's Covered Bridges
Oregon Covered Bridges
Quebec Covered Bridges
The Covered Bridges of Kentucky (eBook)
The Covered Bridges of Kentucky and Tennessee
The Covered Bridges of Tennessee (eBook)

Vermont's Covered Bridges
The Covered Bridges of Virginia (eBook)
The Covered Bridges of Virginia and West Virginia
Washington Covered Bridges (eBook)
The Covered Bridges of West Virginia (eBook)
Wisconsin Covered Bridges (eBook)

Index

* 9 7 8 1 9 2 7 8 3 5 6 1 6 *